W9-AHF-895

The Story of Jesus

JORDAN GRIFFITH

The Story of Jesus

*From the Manger
to the Throne*

*Ellen G. White
Adapted*

REVIEW AND HERALD® PUBLISHING ASSOCIATION
HAGERSTOWN, MD 21740

Copyright 2003 by
Ellen G. White Estate
All rights reserved.

All Scripture quotations in this book are from the New King James Version.
Copyright © 1979, 1980, 1982 by Thomas Nelson, Inc.
Used by permission. All rights reserved.

This book was
Edited by Gerald Wheeler
Copyedited by Jan Schleifer and James Cavil
Designed by Tina Ivany
Cover art by Russ Harlan
Interior illustrations © Review and Herald® Publishing Association. All rights reserved.
Typeset: 13/16 Berkeley

PRINTED IN U.S.A.

07 06 05 04 03   5 4 3 2 1

R&H Cataloging Service
White, Ellen Gould, 1827-1915
    Story of Jesus

      1. Jesus Christ—Biography—Juvenile works.   I. Title.

        232.9

ISBN 0-8280-1765-4

Contents

The Birth of Jesus

In the little town of Nazareth, nestled among the hills of Galilee, was the home of Joseph and Mary. They would become the earthly parents of Jesus.

Joseph was descended from King David. When the Romans sent out a decree to tax the people, he had to go to Bethlehem, the city of David, to pay the tax.

Travel was difficult in those days. Mary, who went with her husband, was very tired as she climbed the hill on which Bethlehem stands.

How she longed for a comfortable place in which to rest! But the inn was already full. The rich and proud had comfortable places to stay, while these humble travelers had to find rest in a building used to shelter cattle.

Joseph and Mary had little of our world's riches, but they had the love of God, and this made them rich in contentment and peace. They were children of the heavenly King, who was about to give them a wonderful honor.

Angels had been watching them during their journey. When night fell and they stopped to rest, the angels stayed with them.

There in that lowly animal shelter Jesus the Savior was born. Mary put Him in a manger, the animals' feeding trough. In that simple cradle lay the Son of God the Highest—He whose presence had filled the courts of heaven with glory.

Before He came to the earth, Jesus was the Commander of the angel hosts. The brightest and most exalted of the angels heralded His glory. They veiled their faces before Him as He sat upon His throne. In His honor they tossed their crowns at His feet, and sang His triumphs as they beheld His greatness.

Yet the glorious Son of God loved us poor human sinners. He took upon Himself the form of a servant, that He might suffer and die for us.

Jesus might have remained at the Father's side, wearing the kingly crown and the royal robe. For our sake, however, He chose to exchange all the wealth of heaven for the poverty of our world. He chose to leave His throne and the angels who loved Him. The adoration of the heavenly throng He chose to exchange for mockery and abuse from wicked human beings. Because of His love for us, He accepted a life of hardship and a shameful death.

All this Christ did to demonstrate how much God loves us. He lived on earth to show how we may honor God by our obedience to His will. He did this so that by following His example we may at last dwell with Him in His heavenly home.

Many of the priests and rulers among God's people were not ready to welcome Jesus. They knew that the Savior would soon come, but they expected Him to be a mighty king who would make them rich and great. The religious leaders could not imagine the Messiah as a helpless child.

So when Christ was born, God did not reveal the glad news to them. He sent it to some shepherds who kept their flocks on the hills around Bethlehem.

They were good men. As they watched their sheep at night they talked together about the promised Savior, and prayed so earnestly for His coming that

God sent bright messengers from His own throne of light to tell them that the Messiah had arrived.

"And behold, an angel of the Lord stood before them, and the glory of the Lord shone around them, and they were greatly afraid. Then the angel said to them, 'Do not be afraid, for behold, I bring you good tidings of great joy which will be to all people. For there is born to you this day in the city of David a Savior, who is Christ the Lord. And this will be the sign to you: You will find a Babe wrapped in swaddling cloths, lying in a manger.'

"And suddenly there was with the angel a multitude of the heavenly host praising God and saying:

"'Glory to God in the highest,
    And on earth peace, goodwill
        toward men!'

"So it was, when the angels had gone away from them into heaven, that the shepherds said to one another, 'Let us now go to Beth-lehem and see this thing that has come to pass, which the Lord has made known to us.' And they came with haste and found Mary and Joseph, and the Babe lying in a manger. Now when they had seen Him, they made widely known the saying which was told them concerning this Child. And all those who heard it marveled at those things which were told them by the shepherds. But Mary kept all these things and pondered them in her heart" (Luke 2:9-19).

2

Jesus Presented in the Temple

Joseph and Mary were Jews and followed the customs of their nation. When Jesus was 6 weeks old, they brought Him to the Lord in the Temple at Jerusalem.

This was according to the law that God had given to Israel. Jesus was to be obedient in all things. So God's own Son, the Prince of heaven, by His example teaches that we should obey.

Parents would present only the firstborn son of each family at the Temple. This ceremony reminded them of an event that had taken place long before.

When the children of Israel were slaves in Egypt, the Lord sent Moses to set them free. He told Moses to go to Pharaoh, king of Egypt, and say:

"'Thus says the Lord: "Israel is My son, My firstborn. So I say to you, let My son go that he may serve Me. But if you refuse to let him go, indeed I will kill your son, your firstborn"'" (Exodus 4:22, 23).

Moses carried this message to the king. But Pharaoh answered, "Who is the Lord, that I should obey His voice to let Israel go? I do not know the Lord, nor will I let Israel go" (Exodus 5:2).

Then the Lord sent fearful plagues upon the Egyptians. The last plague was the death of the firstborn son of every family, from that of the king to the lowliest in the land.

The Lord told Moses that every family of the Israelites must kill a lamb. Then they should put some of its blood upon the doorposts of their house.

This was a sign that the angel of death might pass over all the houses of the Israelites and destroy nobody but the proud and cruel Egyptians.

This blood of the "passover" represented to the Jews the blood of Christ. In due time God would give His dear Son to be slain as the lamb had been, so that all who believed in Him might be saved from everlasting death. The Bible calls Christ our Passover (1 Corinthians 5:7). Through faith we are redeemed by His blood (Ephesians 1:7).

So as each family in Israel brought the oldest son to the Temple, they were to remember how the children had been saved from the plague, and how all might be saved from sin and eternal death. The priest picked up each child presented at the Temple and held him up before the altar.

Thus he was solemnly dedicated to God. Then after the priest gave him back to his mother, the child's name was written in the roll, or book, that contained the names of the firstborn of Israel. So all who are saved by Christ's blood will have their names written in the book of life.

Joseph and Mary brought Jesus to the priest as the law required. Every day fathers and mothers took their children to the Temple. The Temple priest saw nothing different in Joseph and

Mary from the many others. They were just simple working people.

And in the child Jesus he saw only a helpless infant. Little did the priest think that he was then holding in his arms the Savior of the world, the High Priest of the heavenly temple. But he might have known. Had he obeyed God's Word, the Lord would have taught him all about these things.

At this very time two of God's true servants, Simeon and Anna, were in the Temple. Both had grown old in His service. Now God showed them things that He could not reveal to the proud and selfish priests.

God had promised Simeon that he would not die until he had seen the Savior. As soon as he spotted Jesus in the Temple, he knew that the child was the Promised One.

A soft, heavenly light shone on Jesus' face. Simeon, taking the child in his arms, praised God, and said:

"Lord, now You are letting Your servant depart in peace,
According to Your word;
For my eyes have seen Your salvation
Which You have
prepared before the face of all peoples,
A light to bring
revelation to the Gentiles,
And the glory of Your people Israel" (Luke 2:29-32).

Anna, a prophet, "coming in that instant . . . gave thanks to the Lord, and spoke of Him to all those who looked for redemption in Jerusalem" (Luke 2:38).

So it is that God chooses humble people to be His witnesses. Often those whom the world calls great He has to pass by. Too many people are like those priests and religious rulers.

Eager to serve and honor themselves, they think little about serving and honoring God. Therefore He cannot choose them to tell others of His love and mercy.

Mary, the mother of Jesus, pondered Simeon's prophecy. As she looked at the child in her arms and recalled what the shepherds of Bethlehem had said, she was full of grateful joy and bright hope.

Simeon's words reminded her of the prophecy of Isaiah. She knew that those wonderful words spoke about Jesus:

"The people who walked in darkness
Have seen a great light;
Those who dwelt in the land of the shadow of death,
Upon them a light has shined" (Isaiah 9:2).
"For unto us a Child is born,
Unto us a Son is given;
And the government will be upon His shoulder.
And His name will be called
Wonderful, Counselor, Mighty God,
Everlasting Father, Prince of Peace" (verse 6).

3

The Visit of the Wise Men

God wanted people to know about the coming of Christ to earth. The priests should have taught the people to look for the Savior, but they themselves did not know about it.

So God sent angels to tell the shepherds that Christ had been born, and where they might find Him.

So, too, when Jesus' parents presented Him at the Temple, some received Him as the Savior. God had preserved the lives of Simeon and Anna, and they had the joyful privilege of telling others that Jesus was the promised Messiah.

God meant for others, as well as the Jews, to know that Christ had come. In a country far to the east were wise men who had studied the prophecies about the Messiah. They believed that His arrival was near.

The Jews considered these men heathen, but they did not worship idols. They were honest men who wanted to know the truth and to do God's will.

God sees what is in a person's heart. He knew that He could trust these men. They were in a better condition to receive light from heaven than the selfish and proud priests.

The wise men were philosophers. They had studied God's handiwork in nature and had learned to love Him because of what they saw there.

The men loved to watch the wonders of the night sky. If they should spot a new star, they would welcome its appearance as a great event.

On that night when the angels came to the shepherds of Bethlehem, the wise men had noticed a strange light in the sky. It was the glory that surrounded the angels.

By the time this light faded away, they had seen in the heavens what looked like a new star. At once they thought of the prophecy that says, "A Star shall come out of Jacob; a Scepter shall rise out of Israel"

(Numbers 24:17).

Was this star a sign that the Messiah had come? They determined to follow it to see where it would lead them. It guided them to Judea. But when they approached Jerusalem, the star became so dim that they lost track of it.

Supposing that the Jews could at once guide them to the Savior, the wise men went into Jerusalem and said, "'Where is He who has been born King of the Jews? For we have seen His star in the East and have come to worship Him.'

"When Herod the king heard this, he was troubled, and all Jerusalem with him. And when he had gathered all the chief priests and scribes of the people together, he inquired of them where the Christ was to be born.

"So they said to him, 'In Bethlehem of Judea, for thus it is written by the prophet'" (Matthew 2:2-5).

Herod did not want to hear about a king who might someday take his throne. So he took the wise men off by themselves and asked when they had first seen the star. Then he sent them to Bethlehem, saying, "Go and search carefully for the young Child, and when you have found Him, bring back word to me, that I may come and worship Him also" (verse 8).

When the wise men heard this, they again started on their journey. "And behold, the star which they had seen in the East went before them, till it came and stood over where the young Child was" (verse 9).

"When they had come into the house, they saw the young Child with Mary His mother, and fell down and worshiped Him. And when they had opened their treasures, they presented gifts to Him: gold, frankincense, and myrrh" (verse 11).

The wise men brought the most valuable things they had to the Savior. They set an example for each one of us. Many give presents to their earthly friends but have none for the heavenly Friend who has given them every blessing. We should not be like this. To Christ we should bring the best of all we have—of our time, of our money, and of our love.

We may give to Him by aiding the poor and teaching people about the Savior so we can help to save those for whom He died. Such gifts Jesus will always bless.

4

The Flight Into Egypt

Herod had lied when he said that he wanted to worship Jesus. Actually he wanted to find the child so that he could kill Him. The king feared that the Savior would grow up to be a king and take his kingdom from him.

The wise men prepared to return to tell Herod where they had found Jesus. But an angel told them in a dream to take another way home.

"Now when they had departed, behold, an angel of the Lord appeared to Joseph in a dream, saying, 'Arise, take the young Child and His mother, flee to Egypt, and stay there until I bring you word; for Herod will seek the young Child to destroy Him" (Matthew 2:13).

Joseph did not wait until morning but got up at once. Then with Mary and the child he started by night on the long journey.

The wise men had given costly presents to Jesus. In this way God provided money to pay for the trip and their stay in Egypt until they could return to their own land.

Herod was very angry when he found that the wise men had gone home another way. He knew what God had said through His prophet about Christ's coming.

Because of this he knew that God had used the star as a guide for the wise men. Yet he was still determined to destroy Jesus. In his anger he sent soldiers to kill "all the male children who were in Bethlehem . . . , from two years old and under" (verse 16).

How strange that a man should fight against God! What a terrible scene this murder of the innocent children must have been! Herod had done many cruel things before this, but his wicked life would soon come to an end. He died a terrible death.

Joseph and Mary remained in Egypt until after Herod's death. Then the angel came to Joseph and said, "Arise, take the young Child and His mother, and go to the land of Israel, for those who sought the young Child's life are dead" (verse 20).

Joseph had hoped to make his home in Bethlehem, where Jesus had been born. But when he neared Judea he learned that a son of Herod was now ruling in place of his father.

This made Joseph afraid to go there, and he did not know where to live. To help him, God sent an angel to tell him what he should do. Following the directions of the angel, Joseph returned to his old home in Nazareth.

5

Childhood of Jesus

During His childhood Jesus lived in a little mountain village. He was the Son of God and might have had any spot on earth for His home.

Jesus would have honored any place He might have chosen to live. But He did not go to the homes of rich men or the palaces of kings. He chose to dwell among the poor in Nazareth.

Jesus wants the poor to know that He understands their problems. He has shared all the hard things that they have to go through. The Savior can sympathize with them and help them.

Of Jesus in His early years the Bible says: "The Child grew and became strong in spirit, filled with wisdom; and the grace of God was upon Him" (Luke 2:40). "And Jesus increased in wisdom and stature, and in favor with God and men" (verse 52).

His mind was bright and active. Jesus was of quick understanding. He showed a thoughtfulness and wisdom beyond His years. Yet His ways were simple and childlike, and He grew in mind and body just as any other child did.

But Jesus was not in all things the same as other children. He always showed a sweet, unselfish spirit. His willing hands were always ready to serve others. And He was patient and truthful.

Though firm as a rock in standing for the right, He never failed to be gentle and courteous toward all. In His home, and wherever He might be, He was like a cheerful sunbeam.

Jesus was thoughtful and helpful toward the aged and the poor. He showed kindness even to animals. Tenderly He would care for a little wounded bird. Every living thing was happier when He was near.

In the days of Christ, Jewish people carefully educated their children. Their schools were connected with the synagogues, or places of worship. People called the teachers rabbis.

23

Jesus did not go to these schools, for they taught many things that were not true. Instead of God's Word, they studied the ideas of human beings. Often these ideas contradicted what God had taught through His prophets.

God Himself by His Holy Spirit instructed Mary how to bring up His Son. She taught Jesus from the Holy Scriptures, and He learned to read and study them for Himself.

Jesus also loved to explore the wonderful things that God had made on the earth and in the sky. In this book of nature He studied the plants and animals and the sun and the stars.

Day by day He watched them. As He did so He tried to learn lessons from them. He wanted to understand the reason of things.

Holy angels were always with Him. They helped Jesus to learn about God from the things of creation. Thus, as He grew in height and strength, He grew also in knowledge and wisdom.

Every child may gain knowledge just as Jesus did. We should spend our time in learning only that which is true. Falsehood and make-believe will do us no good.

Only the truth is of any value, and this we may learn from God's Word and from His works. As we study these things, the angels will help us to understand.

Then we shall see the wisdom and goodness of our heavenly Father. It will strengthen our minds. The Holy Spirit will make our hearts pure, and we shall be more like Christ.

Every year Joseph and Mary went up to Jerusalem to the feast of Passover. When Jesus was 12 years old they took Him with them.

It was a pleasant journey. The people traveled on foot or rode on donkeys. The trip took several days. The distance from Nazareth to Jerusalem is about 70 miles. From all parts of the land, and even from other countries, the people went to this feast. Those from the same place usually traveled together.

The feast took place near the close of March or the beginning of April. This was springtime in Palestine. The whole land was bright with flowers and happy with the song of birds.

As they traveled parents told their children of the wonderful things that God had done for Israel in the past. And often they sang together some of the beautiful psalms of David.

In the days of Christ the people had grown cold and formal in their service to God. They thought more of their own desires and wants than of His goodness to them.

But it was not so with Jesus. He loved to think about God. As He came to the Temple He watched the priests in their work. He bowed with the worshipers as they knelt to pray. His voice joined in the songs of praise.

Every morning and evening the priests offered a lamb upon the altar. It represented the death of the Savior. As the child Jesus looked upon the innocent victim, the Holy Spirit taught Him its meaning. He began to understand that He Himself, as the Lamb of God, must die for the sins of people.

With such thoughts in His mind Jesus wanted to be alone. So He did not stay with His parents in the Temple. When they started for home He did not go with them.

In a room by the Temple the rabbis had a school. After a while the child Jesus came to sit with the other youth at the feet of the great teachers. There He listened to their words.

The people of Jesus' time had many wrong ideas about the Messiah. Jesus knew this, but He did not contradict the teachers. As one who wished to learn, He asked questions about what the prophets had written.

Isaiah 53 speaks about the Savior's death. Jesus read this chapter and asked about its meaning. The rabbis could give no answer. They began to question Jesus. His knowledge of the Scriptures amazed them.

They saw that He understood the Bible far better than they did. What He said showed them that their teaching was wrong. But they were not willing to believe anything different.

Yet Jesus was so modest and gentle that they were not angry with Him. They wanted to keep Him as a student. Then they could teach Him to explain the Bible as they did.

When Joseph and Mary left Jerusalem on their journey toward home, they did not notice that Jesus had stayed behind. They thought that He was with some of their friends in the group that traveled together.

But when His parents stopped to camp for the night, they missed His helpful hand. They looked for Him everywhere but could not find Him.

Joseph and Mary became afraid. They remembered how Herod had tried to kill Jesus when He was an infant. Now they worried that something bad had happened to Him.

With sorrowful hearts they hurried back to Jerusalem. But it was not till the third day that they found Him.

Although they were glad to see Him again, Mary thought that He was to blame for leaving them. She said:

"'Son, why have You done this to us? Look, Your father and I have sought You anxiously.'

"And He said to them, 'Why did you seek Me? Did you not know that I must be about My Father's business?'" (Luke 2:48, 49).

As He spoke these words Jesus pointed upward. On His face was a light that amazed them. Jesus knew that He was the Son of God and that He had been doing the work His Father had sent Him into the world for.

Mary never forgot these words. In the years that followed she would better understand their wonderful meaning.

Joseph and Mary loved Jesus, yet they had been careless in losing Him. They had forgotten the very work that God had given them to do. By one day's neglect they lost Jesus.

In the same way today many lose the Savior. When we do not love to think about Him or pray to Him, or when we speak idle, unkind, or evil words, we separate ourselves from Christ. Without Him we are lonely and sad.

But if we really want Him to always be with us, He always will. The Savior loves to stay with all who seek His presence. He will brighten the poorest home and gladden the lowliest heart.

Though He knew that He was the Son of God, Jesus went home to Nazareth with Joseph and Mary. He helped His family until He was 30 years of age.

Christ, who had been the Commander of heaven, was on earth a loving and obedient son. The great thoughts brought to His mind by the service of the Temple He now kept hidden in His heart. He waited until God's time to begin His appointed work.

Jesus lived in the home of a poor man. Faithfully and cheerfully He did His part in helping to support the family. As soon as He was old enough He learned a trade and worked in the carpenter's shop with Joseph.

Wearing the coarse clothing of a common laborer, He passed through the streets of the little town, going to and from His work. He did not use His divine power to make His life easier for Himself.

As Jesus worked in childhood and youth He grew strong in body and mind. He tried to use all His powers in such a way as to keep them in health, that He might do the best work, no matter what it was.

Whatever He did was done well. He wanted to be perfect, even when using tools. By His example He taught that we ought to be industrious, that we should do our work carefully and well. His life showed that work is honorable. All should find something to do that will be helpful to themselves and to others.

God gave us work as a blessing. It makes Him happy when children cheerfully take their part in household tasks and share the burdens of father and mother. Such children will leave home to be a blessing to others.

Young people who try to please God in all that they do, who do right because it is right, will be useful in the world. By being faithful in a humble place, they prepare themselves for a higher position.

6

Days of Conflict

The religious teachers made many rules for the people. They required them to do many things that God had not commanded. Even children had to obey such rules. But Jesus did not try to learn what the rabbis taught. Instead, He studied only the Scriptures and obeyed only God's laws. Still, He was careful not to speak disrespectfully about the teachers.

Often people scolded Him for not doing what others did. Then He showed from the Bible what was the right way.

Jesus always tried to make others happy. Because He was so kind and gentle, the rabbis hoped to make Him do as they did. But they could not change Him. When they urged Him to obey their rules He would ask what the Bible taught. Whatever that said, He told them, He would do.

This made the rabbis angry. They knew that their rules were contrary to the Bible, and yet they were angry with Jesus for refusing to obey them.

They complained about Him to His parents. Joseph and Mary thought the rabbis were good men. They scolded Jesus for not obeying. It was hard for Jesus to bear.

The brothers of Jesus took sides with the rabbis. The words of these teachers, they said, should be obeyed as the Word of God. They criticized Jesus for setting Himself above the leaders of the people.

Some rabbis thought themselves better than other people. They would not associate with ordinary people and despised the poor and uneducated. And they refused to help even the sick and suffering.

Jesus showed a loving interest in everybody. He tried to help every suffering person. Because He had little money to give, He often went without food so that He could give to others the money He would have used to buy it.

When His brothers spoke harshly to anyone, Jesus would go to the person and speak words of kindness and encouragement.

To those who were hungry and thirsty He would bring a cup of cold water. Often He would give them food from His own meal.

All this angered His brothers. They threatened Him, but He kept right on doing as God wanted Him to.

Jesus had to face many trials and temptations. Satan was always trying to overcome Him.

If Jesus had done one wrong act or spoken one impatient word, He could not have been our Savior. The whole world would have been lost. Satan knew this, and it was for this reason that he tried so hard to lead Jesus into sin.

Heavenly angels always guarded Jesus, yet His life was one long struggle against the powers of darkness. Not one of us will ever have to meet such fierce temptations as He did.

But to every temptation He had one answer: "It is written." He did not often rebuke the wrongdoing of His brothers, but He did tell them what God had said was the right thing to do.

Nazareth was a wicked town. Its children and young people tried to make Jesus follow their evil ways. He was bright and cheerful, and they liked His company.

But His godly principles made them angry. Often they called Him a coward for refusing to join in some forbidden act. They would sneer at Him for being too particular about little things. To all this He would answer from the Scriptures: "'Behold, the fear of the Lord, that is wisdom, and to depart from evil is understanding'" (Job 28:28). To love evil is to love death, for "the wages of sin is death" (Romans 6:23).

Jesus did not fight for His rights. When people abused Him, He bore it patiently.

30

Because He was so willing and uncomplaining, it made His work needlessly hard. Yet He was not discouraged, for He knew that God smiled upon Him.

His happiest hours He spent alone with nature and with God. When He finished His work, He loved to go into the fields and green valleys to think and meditate. He would pray to God on the mountainside or amid the trees of the forest.

Jesus listened to the lark singing to its Creator, and His voice joined the song of joyful praise and thanksgiving.

With singing He welcomed the morning light. The break of day often found Him in some quiet place, thinking about God, studying the Bible, or talking to God in prayer.

From these peaceful hours He would return home to take up His duties again and to give an example of patient toil.

Wherever He was, His presence seemed to bring the angels near. All classes of people felt the influence of His pure, holy life.

Harmless and undefiled, He walked among the thoughtless, the rude, and the discourteous. He met the unjust tax collectors, the pagan Roman soldiers, and the rough peasants.

Jesus constantly spoke words of sympathy to those bearing heavy loads. He shared their burdens and repeated to them the lessons He had learned from nature about the love, kindness, and goodness of God.

He taught them to look upon themselves as having valuable talents. By His own example He taught that every moment of time is precious and should be put to some good use.

He considered no human being as worthless, but tried to encourage even the roughest and most unpromising. He told them that God loved them as His children and that they might become like Him in character.

So in a quiet way Jesus worked for others from the time He was a child. Neither the learned teachers nor His own brothers could make Him give up this work. With great dedication He carried out the purpose of His life, for He was to be the light of the world.

7

The Baptism

When the time for Christ's public ministry had come, His first act was to go to the Jordan River and be baptized by John the Baptist.

John had been sent to prepare the way for the Savior. He had preached in the desert, saying:

"Repent, for the kingdom of heaven is at hand!" (Matthew 3:2).

Multitudes flocked to hear him. Many were convicted of their sins, and John baptized them in the Jordan.

God had made known to John that some day the Messiah would come to him and ask to be baptized. The Lord had also promised that John would receive a sign so that he might know who the Messiah was.

When Jesus came, John saw in His face such signs of His holy life that he tried

to stop Him, saying: "'I need to be baptized by You, and are You coming to me?'

"But Jesus answered and said to him, 'Permit it to be so now, for thus it is fitting for us to fulfill all righteousness'" (Matthew 3:14, 15).

And as He said this, John noticed upon His face the same heavenly light that Simeon had seen.

So John led the Savior down into the waters of the muddy Jordan. There he baptized Him in the sight of all the people.

Jesus was not baptized to show repentance for His own sins, because He had never sinned. He did it to set an example for us.

When He came up out of the water, He kneeled on the riverbank and prayed. Then the heavens opened and beams of glory streamed forth. Jesus "saw the Spirit of God descending like a dove and alighting upon Him" (verse 16).

His face and body were all aglow with the light of the glory of God. And He heard the voice of God saying from heaven:

"This is My beloved Son, in whom I am well pleased" (verse 17).

The glory that rested upon Christ was

a pledge of God's love for us. The Savior came as our example, and just as surely as God heard His prayer, He will hear ours.

The most needy, the most sinful, the most despised, may find an open door to the Father. When we come to Him in Jesus' name, the voice that spoke to Jesus also speaks to us, saying: "This is My beloved child, in whom I am well pleased."

8

The Temptation

After His baptism Christ was led by the Spirit into the wilderness to face temptation from the devil.

Christ did not look for temptation. He wanted to be alone so that He might think about His mission and work.

By prayer and fasting He would prepare Himself for the bloodstained path that He must travel. But Satan knew where the Savior had gone, so he went there to tempt Him. As Christ left the Jordan, the glory of God shone on His face. But after He entered the wilderness, it disappeared.

The sins of the world became a heavy burden upon His shoulders. His face showed more sorrow and anguish than any person had ever felt before. He was suffering for sinners—for you and me.

Adam and Eve in Eden had disobeyed God by eating the forbidden fruit. Their disobedience had brought sin and sorrow and death into our world.

Christ came to give an example of obedience. In the wilderness, after fasting 40 days, He would not depart from the will of His Father even to obtain food.

One of the temptations that overcame our first parents was the desire to indulge hunger. By His long fast Christ showed that we can bring it under control.

Satan tempts people to overindulge in things because this weakens the body and clouds the mind. He knows that then he can then more easily deceive and destroy them.

But Christ's example teaches that every wrong desire must be overcome. Such desires should not rule us—we must rule them.

When Satan first appeared to Christ, he looked like an angel. He claimed to be a messenger from heaven.

Satan told Jesus that His Father did not want Him to go through such suffering. Christ had to show only a willingness to suffer.

When Jesus was struggling against the keenest pangs of hunger, Satan said to Him:

"If You are the Son of God, command that these stones become bread" (Matthew 4:3).

But since the Savior had come to live as our example, He must endure suffering as we have to endure it. Thus He must not work a miracle for His own good. His miracles were all to be for the good of others. To the demand of Satan He answered:

"It is written, 'Man shall not live by bread alone, but by every word that proceeds from the mouth of God'" (verse 4).

Thus He showed that it is far less important to provide ourselves with food than it is to obey the Word of God. Those who obey God's Word have the promise of anything that they might need for the present life. Also they have God's promise of the future life.

Satan had failed to overcome Christ in the first great temptation. Next he carried Him to a pinnacle of the Temple at Jerusalem and said:

"If You are the Son of God, throw Yourself down. For it is written: 'He shall give His angels charge over you,' and, 'In their hands they shall bear you up, Lest you dash your foot against a stone'" (verse 6).

Satan here followed Christ's example in quoting Scripture. But God did not make this promise for those who deliberately get themselves into danger. God had not told Jesus to throw Himself down from the Temple. Jesus would not do it to please Satan. He told the devil: "It is written again, 'You shall not tempt the Lord your God'" (verse 7).

We should trust in the care of our heavenly Father, but we

must not go where He does not send us. We must not do what He has forbidden.

Because God is merciful and ready to forgive, some people will say that it is safe to disobey Him and then ask forgiveness. But this is presumption. God will forgive all who seek pardon and turn away from sin. But those who deliberately choose to disobey Him, He can not bless.

Satan now appeared as what he really was—the prince of the powers of darkness. He took Jesus to the top of a high mountain and showed Him all the world's kingdoms.

The sunlight shimmered on splendid cities, marble palaces, fruitful fields and vineyards. Satan said:

"All these things I will give You if You will fall down and worship me" (verse 9).

For a moment Christ looked upon the wonderful scene. Then He turned away. Satan had presented the world to Him in the most attractive light, but the Savior saw beneath the outward beauty.

He saw the world apart from God in its wretchedness and sin. All this misery was the result of people turning away from God to worship Satan.

A longing to redeem that which was lost filled Christ. He wanted to restore the world to more than the beauty it had in Eden. He wanted to place human beings on higher ground with God.

Christ was resisting temptation so He could save the human race. He was to be an overcomer, that human beings might also overcome, that they might be equal with the angels, and be worthy to be acknowledged as children of God.

To Satan's demand for worship Christ answered:

"Away with you, Satan! For it is written, 'You shall worship the Lord your God, and Him only you shall serve'" (verse 10).

The love of the world, the lust for power, and the pride of life—everything that draws human beings away from the worship of God—Satan used to try to tempt Christ.

Satan offered Christ the world and its riches if He would pay homage to the principles of evil. In the same way, Satan presents to us the advantages to be gained by wrongdoing.

He whispers to us, "In order to succeed in this world you must serve me. Do not be too particular about truth and honesty. Do what I say, and I will give you riches, honor, and happiness."

But when we do that, we are worshiping Satan instead of God. It will bring us only misery and ruin.

Christ has shown us what we should do when tempted.

When He said to Satan, "Away with you," the devil could not resist the command. He had no choice but to go.

Writhing with baffled hate and rage, the rebel chief left the presence of the world's Redeemer.

The contest ended for the moment. Christ's victory was as complete as had been Adam's failure.

So we also may resist temptation and overcome Satan. The Lord says to us: "Resist the devil and he will flee from you. Draw near to God and He will draw near to you" (James 4:7, 8).

9

Early Ministry

Returning from the wilderness, Christ went back to the Jordan, where John the Baptist was preaching. At that time men sent by the rulers in Jerusalem were questioning John about his authority for teaching and baptizing the people.

They asked if he was the Messiah, or Elijah, or "that prophet," meaning Moses. To all this he answered, "I am not."

Then they asked:

"Who are you, that we may give an answer to those who sent us?" (John 1:22).

"He said, 'I am "The voice of one crying in the wilderness: 'Make straight the way of the Lord,'" as the prophet Isaiah said'" (verse 23).

In old times when a king had to travel from one part of his country to another, he sent people ahead of his chariot to prepare the roads.

They had to cut down trees, remove stones, and fill up the hollows so that the way would be clear for the king.

So when Jesus, the heavenly King, was coming, God sent John the Baptist to prepare the way by telling the people about Him and urging them to repent of their sins.

As John answered the messengers from Jerusalem he saw Jesus standing on the riverbank. His face lighted up, and, stretching out his hands, he said: "There stands One among you whom you do not know. It is He who, coming after me, is preferred before me, whose sandal strap I am not worthy to loose"

(verses 26, 27).

The people became greatly excited. The Messiah was among them! They looked around eagerly to find the one John had spoken about. But Jesus had disappeared into the crowd and disappeared from sight.

The next day John again saw Jesus and, pointing to Him, shouted, "Behold! The Lamb of God who takes away the sin of the world!" (verse 29).

Then John told of the sign that he had seen at Christ's baptism. "I have seen and testified that this is the Son of God" (verse 34).

With awe and wonder his audience looked at Jesus. They asked themselves, "Is this the Christ?"

They saw that Jesus bore no signs of worldly wealth or greatness. His clothing was plain and simple, such as poor people wore. But in His pale, worn face they spotted something that moved their hearts.

In that face they read dignity and power. Every glance of the eye, every expression, spoke of divine compassion and unutterable love.

But the messengers from Jerusalem were not drawn to the Savior. John had not said what they desired to hear. They expected the Messiah to come as a great conqueror. But they quickly saw that this was not Jesus' mission. In disappointment they turned away from Him.

The next day John again saw Jesus, and again he cried, "Behold the Lamb of God!" (verse 36). Two of John's disciples were standing nearby, and they decided to follow Jesus. They listened to His teaching and became His disciples. One of the two was Andrew, the other John.

Andrew soon brought to Jesus his own brother, Simon, whom Christ named Peter. The next day on the way to Galilee Christ called another disciple, Philip. As soon as Philip met the Savior, he brought his friend Nathanael.

In this way Christ's great work on earth began. One by one He called His disciples. One then brought his brother, another his friend. This is what all followers of Christ are to do. As soon as they know Jesus they must tell others what a wonderful Friend they have found. This is a work that all can do, whether they are young or old.

At Cana in Galilee Christ, with His disciples, attended a marriage feast. To make the gathering happy, He performed a miracle.

The feast had run out of wine. Those who knew the wine was gone realized that if the guests learned about it, they would consider it a lack of hospitality. It would bring a great disgrace on the family.

When Christ was told what had happened, He told the servants to fill six large stone jars with water. Then He said, "Draw some out now, and take it to the master of the feast" (John 2:8).

Instead of water, the jars now had wine in them. This wine was much better than that served before, and there was enough for all.

After working the miracle, Jesus quietly went away. Not till He had gone did the guests learn what He had done.

Christ's gift to the marriage feast was a symbol. The water represented baptism. The wine was His blood that He would shed for the world.

The wine that Jesus made was not fermented. Alcohol causes drunkenness and many great evils, and God had forbidden its use. He says: "Wine is a mocker, strong drink is a brawler, and whoever is led astray by it is not wise" (Proverbs 20:1). "At the last it bites like a serpent, and stings like a viper" (Proverbs 23:32).

The wine used at the feast was the pure, sweet juice of the grape. It was like that which the prophet Isaiah calls "the new wine . . . in the cluster;" and he says, "A blessing is in it" (Isaiah 65:8).

By going to the marriage feast, Christ showed that it is right to meet together in this pleasant way. He liked to see people happy. Often He visited them in their homes and tried to help them forget their cares and their troubles. Jesus wanted them to think of God's goodness and His love. No matter where He might be, Christ was always trying to do this. Wherever a heart was open to receive the divine message, He unfolded the truths of the way of salvation.

One day, as He was passing through the country of Samaria, He sat down by a well to rest. When a woman came to get water from it, He asked her for a drink.

The woman wondered about this, for she knew how the Jews hated the

Samaritans. But Christ told her that if she would just ask for it from Him, He would give her living water. This amazed her even more.

Then Jesus said to her:

"Whoever drinks of this water will thirst again, but whoever drinks of the water that I shall give him will never thirst. But the water that I shall give him will become in him a fountain of water springing up into everlasting life" (John 4:13, 14).

By the living water Jesus meant the Holy Spirit. As a thirsty traveler needs water to drink, so we need God's Spirit in our hearts. He who drinks of this water will never have any spiritual thirst.

The Holy Spirit brings God's love into our hearts. It satisfies our longings. The riches and honors and pleasures of this world will then not attract us.

And it fills us with such joy that we want others to have it too. It will be in us like a spring of water that bubbles out in blessing to everyone around us.

And everyone in whom God's Spirit dwells will live forever with Christ in His kingdom. When we receive the Spirit into our hearts by faith, it is the beginning of eternal life.

Christ told the woman He would give her this precious blessing if she asked for it. And He will give it to us, too.

Christ gently showed her that He knew the sins in her life. But He showed, too, that He was her friend, that He loved her, and that if she was willing to forsake her sins, God would accept her as His child.

How glad she was to know this! In her joy she hurried to the town nearby. There she urged the people to come and see Jesus.

So they hurried to the well and asked Him to stay with them. He remained two days and taught them. Many listened carefully to His words. They repented of their sins and believed that He was the Savior.

During His ministry Jesus twice visited His old home in Nazareth. On the first visit He went to the synagogue on Sabbath.

Here He read from Isaiah's prophecy about the work of the Messiah—how He was to preach good tidings to the poor, to comfort the sorrowing, to give sight to the blind, and to heal those that had been bruised by life.

Then He told the people that all this was being fulfilled that day. This was the work that He Himself was doing.

Joy filled His hearers. They believed that Jesus was the promised Savior. The Holy Spirit moved their hearts, and they responded with praise to the Lord.

Then they remembered how Jesus had lived among them as a carpenter. Often they had seen Him working in the shop with Joseph. Although His whole life had been one of constant deeds of love and mercy, they would not believe that He was the Messiah.

Such thoughts opened the way for Satan to control their minds. Becoming angry at the Savior, they decided to kill Him.

Seizing Him, they tried to throw Him over the steep side of a hill. But angels protected Jesus. He passed safely through the crowd and left.

The next time He came to Nazareth, the people still were not ready to accept Him. This time He went away never to return.

Christ worked for those who wanted His help. All throughout the countryside the people flocked about Him. As He healed and taught them, there was great rejoicing. Heaven seemed to come down to the earth as they basked in the love of a merciful Savior.

10

Teachings of Christ

Religion had come to be little more than a round of ceremonies among many of the people in Jesus' time. As they forgot how to truly worship God, they lost the spiritual power of His Word. They had tried to make up for it through ceremonies and traditions of their own.

Only the blood of Christ can cleanse from sin. Only His power can keep us from sinning. But many of the people depended upon their own efforts and the ceremonies of their religion to earn salvation. Because of their zeal for these ceremonies they thought themselves worthy of a place in God's kingdom.

But they had set their hopes on worldly greatness. They expected riches and power as the reward for their pretended piety.

The people thought that the Messiah would set up His kingdom on this earth and rule as a mighty prince. At His coming they hoped to receive every worldly blessing.

Jesus knew that they would be disappointed. He had come to teach them about something far better.

Christ had come to restore the true worship of God. He would bring in a pure religion of the heart that would reveal itself in a pure life and a holy character.

In the beautiful Sermon on the Mount He explained what would give people real happiness.

The teachings of the rabbis had influenced Jesus' disciples. It was to them, first of all, that Christ presented His lessons. But they are for us, also. We need to learn the same things.

"Blessed are the poor in spirit," Christ said (Matthew 5:3). The poor in spirit are those who know their own sinfulness and need. They realize that they can do nothing good without God's help. Now they desire help from God, and to them He gives His blessing.

"For thus says the High and Lofty One who inhabits eternity, whose name is Holy: 'I dwell in the high and holy place, with him who has a contrite and humble spirit, to revive the spirit of the humble, and to revive the heart of the contrite ones'" (Isaiah 57:15).

"Blessed are those who mourn" (Matthew 5:4). This does not mean those who complain and murmur, who go about with a sour expression. It means those who are truly sorry for their sins and who ask God for forgiveness.

He will freely forgive every such person. He says, "I will turn their mourning to joy, will comfort them, and make them rejoice rather than sorrow" (Jeremiah 31:13).

"Blessed are the meek," Christ said (Matthew 5:5). "Learn from Me, for I am gentle and lowly in heart" (Matthew 11:29). When others did bad things to Him, Jesus responded only with good. He set an example of what we should do.

"Blessed are those who hunger and thirst for righteousness" (Matthew 5:6). Righteousness is right-doing. It is obeying God's law. God's law teaches us the principles of righteousness. The Bible tells us that "all Your commandments are righteousness" (Psalm 119:172).

That law Christ, by His example, taught us how to obey. We see the righteousness of the law in His life. We hunger and thirst after righteousness when we want to have all our thoughts, our words, and our actions like those of Christ.

And we may be like Christ if we really desire to be. We may have our lives like His life, our actions in harmony with God's law. The Holy Spirit will bring God's love into our hearts so that we shall do His will with delight.

God is more willing to give us His Spirit than parents are to give good things to their children. His promise is: "Ask, and it will be given to you" (Luke 11:9; Matthew 7:7). All those who hunger and thirst after righteousness "shall be filled" (Matthew 5:6).

"Blessed are the merciful" (Matthew 5:7). To be merciful is to treat others better than they deserve. That is the way God does with us. He delights to show mercy. God is kind even to unthankful and evil persons.

So He teaches us to treat one another the same way that He does. He says, "Be kind to one another, tender hearted, forgiving one another, even as God in Christ forgave you" (Ephesians 4:32).

"Blessed are the pure in heart" (Matthew 5:8). God cares more for what we really are than for what we claim to be. He wants our hearts to be pure. Then all our words and actions will be right.

King David prayed, "Create in me a clean heart, O God" (Psalm 51:10). "Let the words of my mouth and the meditation of my heart be acceptable in Your sight, O Lord, my strength and my Redeemer" (Psalm 19:14). This should be our prayer.

"Blessed are the peacemakers" (Matthew 5:9). He who has the meek and lowly spirit of Christ will be a peacemaker. Such a spirit does not start quarrels or respond in anger. It makes the home happy and brings a sweet peace that blesses all around.

"Blessed are those who are persecuted for righteousness' sake" (Matthew 5:10). Christ knew that for His sake many of His disciples would be put in prison and many would be killed. But He told them not to get upset because of this.

Nothing can harm those who love and follow Christ. He will be with them no matter where they are. They may be put to death, but He will give them a life that will never end.

And from them others will learn about the Savior. Christ said to His disciples: "You are the light of the world" (Matthew 5:14). Jesus would return to His heavenly home. But the disciples were to teach the people of His love. They were to be as lights among the human race.

The lamp in the lighthouse, shining out in the darkness, guides the ship safely to the harbor. In the same way, Christ's followers are to shine in this dark world, to guide others to Christ and the heavenly home.

This is what all the followers of Christ are to do. He calls them to work with

Russ Harlan

Him in saving others.

Such lessons were strange and new to Christ's hearers. He had to repeat them many times.

Once a religious leader came to Him with this question: "Teacher, what shall I do to inherit eternal life?" (Luke 10:25).

Jesus "said to him, 'What is written in the law? What is your reading of it?'

"So he answered and said, '"You shall love the Lord your God with all your heart, with all your soul, with all your strength, and with all your mind," and "your neighbor as yourself."'

"And He said to him, 'You have answered rightly; do this and you will live'" (verses 26-28).

But the religious leader had not done this. He knew that he had not loved others as himself. Instead of repenting, he tried to find an excuse for his selfishness. So he asked Jesus, "Who is my neighbor?" (verse 29).

The priests and rabbis often argued about this question. They did not consider the poor and uneducated as their neighbors and would show them no kindness. Christ took no part in their disputes, but He did answer the question by a story about something that had happened a short time before.

A certain man, He said, traveled from Jerusalem to Jericho. The road was steep and rocky and passed through a wild, lonely region. Robbers attacked the man and stripped him of all that he had. After beating him up, they left him for dead.

As he lay there a priest and then a Levite from the Temple at Jerusalem went by. But instead of helping the poor man, they walked around him.

God had chosen these men to serve in His Temple. They ought to have been like Him, full of mercy and kindness. But their hearts were cold and unfeeling.

After a while a Samaritan came by. The Jews hated and despised the Samaritans. They would not give them so much as a drink of water or a bite of bread. But the Samaritan did not stop to think of this. He did not stop even to think about the robbers who might be watching for him.

There lay the stranger, bleeding and ready to die. The Samaritan took off his own cloak and wrapped it about the man.

He gave the robbery victim his own wine to drink and poured olive oil on his wounds. Then he put the man on his own donkey, brought him to an inn, and took care of him all night.

The next morning, before going on his way, he paid the innkeeper to care for the injured man till he should be strong again. After Jesus told the story, He turned to the religious leader.

"So which of these three do you think was neighbor to him who fell among the thieves?" (verse 36).

The lawyer answered, "He who showed mercy on him" (verse 37).

Then Jesus said, "Go and do likewise" (verse 37). So Jesus taught that every person who needs our help is our neighbor. We are to treat them just as we ourselves would like to be treated.

The priest and the Levite pretended to keep God's commandments, but it was the Samaritan who really obeyed them. His heart was kind and loving.

By taking care of the wounded stranger, he was showing love to God as well as to his fellow human beings. It pleases God to have us do good to one another. We show our love for Him by being kind to those about us.

A kind, loving heart is worth more than all the riches in the world. Those who live to do good show that they are God's children. They are the ones who will dwell with Christ in His kingdom.

11

Sabbathkeeping

The Savior kept the Sabbath and taught His disciples to honor it. He knew how it should be kept, for He Himself had made it holy.

The Bible says: "Remember the Sabbath day, to keep it holy" (Exodus 20:8). "The seventh day is the Sabbath of the Lord your God" (verse 10). "For in six days the Lord made the heavens and the earth, the sea, and all that is in them, and rested the seventh day. Therefore the Lord blessed the Sabbath day and hallowed it" (verse 11).

Christ had worked with His Father in creating the earth, and He had made the Sabbath. The Bible says that "all things were made through Him" (John 1:3).

When we look at the sun and the stars, the trees and the beautiful flowers, we should remember that Christ made them all. And He made the Sabbath to help us keep in mind His love and power.

The religious teachers had made many rules about the way to keep the Sabbath, and they wanted everyone to obey their rules. So they watched the Savior to see what He would do.

One Sabbath as Christ and His disciples were going home from the synagogue, they passed through a field of grain. It was late, and the disciples were hungry. So they broke off some of the heads of grain, rubbed them between their hands, and ate the kernels.

On any other day anyone passing through a field or an orchard was allowed to gather what he or she wanted to eat. But it was not so on the Sabbath. Christ's enemies saw what the disciples were doing. They said to the Savior: "Look, Your disciples are doing what is not lawful to do on the Sabbath!" (Matthew 12:2).

But Christ defended His disciples. He reminded His accusers of David, who, when in need, had eaten the sacred bread of the tabernacle. He had even given it to his hungry followers.

If it was right for David to eat this sacred bread when hungry, then was it not right for the disciples to pluck the grain on the sacred hours of the Sabbath when hungry?

God had not meant the Sabbath to be a burden to people. It was to do them good, to give them peace and rest. Therefore our Lord said, "The Sabbath was made for man, and not man for the Sabbath" (Mark 2:27).

"Now it happened on another Sabbath, also, that He entered the synagogue and taught. And a man was there whose right hand was withered. So the scribes and Pharisees watched Him closely, whether He would heal on the Sabbath, that they might find an accusation against Him. But He knew their thoughts, and said to the man who had the withered hand, 'Arise and stand here.' And he arose and stood. Then Jesus said to them, 'I will ask you one thing: Is it lawful on the Sabbath to do good or to do evil, to save life or to destroy?' And when He had looked around at them all, He said to the man, 'Stretch out your hand.' And he did so, and his hand was restored as whole as the other. But they were filled with rage, and discussed with one another what they might do to Jesus" (Luke 6:6-11).

The Savior showed how unreasonable they were about the way they kept

Sabbath by one time asking them a question. "What man is there among you who has one sheep, and if it falls into a pit on the Sabbath, will not lay hold of it and lift it out?" (Matthew 12:11).

They could not answer. So He said, "Of how much more value then is a man than a sheep? Therefore it is lawful to do good on the Sabbath" (Matthew 12:12).

"It is lawful"—that is, it is according to law. Christ never reproved the Jews for keeping the law of God or for honoring the Sabbath. On the contrary, He always upheld the law in all its completeness.

Isaiah prophesied of Christ, "He will exalt the law and make it honorable" (Isaiah 42:21). To exalt something is to raise it to a higher position.

Christ exalted the law by showing in every part its wonderful meaning. He demonstrated that it is to be obeyed, not only in actions that others can see but also in the thoughts, something known only to God.

To those who claimed that He came to get rid of the law, He said, "Do not think that I came to destroy the Law or the Prophets. I did not come to destroy but to fulfill" (Matthew 5:17).

To fulfill means to obey or to put into action. So when He came to be baptized by John the Baptist, He said, "For thus it is fitting for us to fulfill all righteousness" (Matthew 3:15). To fulfill the law is to obey it.

God's law can never be changed. Christ said, "Till heaven and earth pass away, one jot or one tittle will by no means pass from the law till all is fulfilled" (Matthew 5:18).

When He asked the question "Is it lawful on the Sabbath to do good or to do evil, to save life or to destroy it?" Christ showed that He could read the hearts of the wicked people who accused Him of breaking the Sabbath.

While He was trying to save life by healing the sick, they were trying to destroy life by putting Him to death. Was it better to slay upon the Sabbath, as they were planning to do, than to cure suffering, as He had done?

Was it better to have murder in the heart on God's holy day than to have love toward all people—love shown in kindness and deeds of mercy?

Many times religious leaders charged Christ with breaking the Sabbath. Often they tried to kill Him because He did not keep it according to their ways. But this made no difference with Him. He observed the Sabbath as God wanted it to be kept.

Jerusalem had a large pool of water called Bethesda. At certain times something disturbed the water in it. Some people believed that an angel went down into it and stirred the waters. The first one who then stepped into the waters would be cured of whatever disease he or she had.

Great numbers of people came to the place, hoping to be cured. Most of them would be disappointed. Because of the crowd many could not even get to the edge of the pool.

One Sabbath Jesus visited Bethesda. His heart filled with pity as He saw the suffering people there.

He noticed one man who seemed more wretched than the others. For 38 years he had been a helpless cripple. No doctor could cure him. Many times friends had brought him to Bethesda, but when the waters stirred, another would step in before him.

On this Sabbath he had tried once more to reach the pool, but in vain. Jesus saw him as he crept back to the mat that was his bed. The man's strength was almost gone. Unless help should come soon, he would die.

As he lay there, now and then lifting his eyes to look at the pool, a loving face bent over him. He heard a voice say, "Do you want to be made well?" (John 5:6).

The man answered sorrowfully, "Sir, I have no man to put me into the pool when the water is stirred up; but while I am coming, another steps down before me" (verse 7).

He did not know that the one beside him could heal—not him only, but all who should come to Him. Christ said to the man, "Rise, take up your bed and walk" (verse 8).

Instantly he tried to obey the command. He sprang to his feet and found that he could stand and walk.

Picking up his bed, he hurried away, praising God at every step. Soon he met

some of the Pharisees and told them of his wonderful cure. They did not seem glad but scolded him for carrying his bed on the Sabbath. The man tried to explain why he was doing it. "He who made me well said to me, 'Take up your bed and walk'" (John 5:11).

Then the religious leaders blamed the one who had told him to carry his bed on the Sabbath.

Many of the learned rabbis lived in Jerusalem and taught their false ideas about the Sabbath there. Great numbers of people came to worship at the Temple. They then spread the rabbis' teaching far and wide. Christ wished to correct such errors. This was why He healed the man on the Sabbath and told him to carry his bed. He knew that it would attract the attention of the rabbis and give Him an opportunity to instruct them. The Pharisees brought Christ before the Sanhedrin, the chief council of the Jews, to question Him about what they considered His Sabbathbreaking.

The Savior declared that what He had done did not break the Sabbath law. It was in harmony with the will and the work of God. "My Father has been working until now," He said, "and I have been working" (John 5:17).

God continually sustains every living thing. Should His work cease upon Sabbath? Should God forbid the sun to fulfill its office on the Sabbath? Should He cut off its rays from warming the earth and nourishing vegetation?

Should the brooks refuse to water the fields, and the waves of the sea stop their ebbing and flowing? Must the wheat and maize stop growing, and the trees and flowers put forth no bud or blossom on the Sabbath?

Then we would miss the fruits of the earth and the other blessings that sustain our lives. Nature must continue her work, or the human race would die. And we also have work to do on this day. We must take care of the necessities of life, care for the sick, and provide for the wants of the needy. God does not desire His creatures to suffer an hour's pain that may be relieved on the Sabbath or any other day.

Heaven's work never ceases, and we should never rest from doing good. Our own work, though, God's law forbids us to do on the Lord's rest day. Our toil for a livelihood must cease. We must not labor for worldly pleasure or profit upon that day. But we must not spend the Sabbath in useless inactivity. As God ceased from His labor of creating and rested upon the Sabbath, so we are to rest. He asks us to lay aside our daily occupations and devote those sacred hours to healthful rest, to worship, and to holy deeds.

12

The Good Shepherd

The Savior spoke of Himself as a shepherd and the disciples as His flock. He said, "I am the good shepherd; and I know My sheep, and am known by My own" (John 10:14).

Christ would soon leave His disciples, and He said this to give them comfort. Then, when He should no longer be with them, they would remember His words.

Whenever they saw a shepherd watching his flock, the disciples would think of the Savior's love and care for them.

In that land the shepherd stayed with his flock day and night. Over the rocky hills and through the forests he led them by day to pleasant grassy fields. Then through the night he guarded them from the wild beasts and robbers that were often lurking nearby.

Tenderly he cared for the feeble and sickly ones. The little lambs he took in his arms and carried against his chest.

However large the flock, the shepherd would know every sheep. He had a name for each animal and called it by its name.

So Christ, the heavenly Shepherd, cares for His flock scattered throughout the world. He knows us all by name. He knows the very house in which we live and the name of each person there. Christ cares for each one as if there were not another person in the whole world.

The shepherd went before his sheep and met all the dangers. He encountered the wild beasts and the robbers. Sometimes the shepherd was killed while guarding his flock.

So the Savior guards His flock of disciples. He has gone before us. Jesus has lived on earth, as we live. First He was a child, then a youth, finally a man. He overcame Satan and all his temptations so that we may also overcome.

Jesus died to save us. Though now He is in heaven, He does not forget us for a moment. He will safely keep every sheep. Not one person that follows Him can be taken by the great enemy.

A shepherd might have 100 sheep, but if one was missing, he did not stay with those already in the sheepfold. He went to search for the lost animal.

Out in the dark night, through the storm, over mountains and valleys, he would go. He would not rest until he had found the sheep.

Then he took it in his arms and carried it back to the fold. The shepherd did not complain of the long, hard search but gladly told others, "Rejoice with me, for I have found my sheep which was lost!" (Luke 15:6).

So the Savior-Shepherd's love and concern is not for only those who are in the fold. He says, "The Son of Man has come to save that which was lost" (Matthew 18:11).

"I say to you that likewise there will be more joy in heaven over one sinner who repents than over ninety-nine just persons who need no repentance" (Luke 15:7).

We have all sinned and wandered away from God. Christ says that we are like

the sheep that has wandered away from the sheepfold. He came to help us live without sin. He calls this bringing us back to the fold.

When we turn away from sin and return with the Shepherd, Christ says to the angels in heaven: "Rejoice with Me, for I have found My sheep which was lost."

And a joyful song rings out from the angelic choir, filling all heaven with richest melody.

Christ presents to us no picture of a sorrowful shepherd returning without the sheep. Here is a pledge that not even one of the straying sheep of God's fold gets overlooked.

Not one goes unhelped. The Savior will rescue from the wilds of sin all those who let Him save them.

Then let every wanderer from the fold take courage. The Good Shepherd is searching for you. Remember that His work is "to save that which is lost." That means you.

To doubt the possibility of your salvation is to doubt the saving power of Him who purchased you at an infinite cost. Let faith take the place of unbelief. Look at the hands that were pierced by nails for you, and rejoice in their power to save.

Remember that God and Christ are interested in you and that all heaven is busy working for the salvation of sinners.

While Christ was on earth He showed by His miracles that He had power to save. By curing the diseases of the body, He showed that He was able to take away sin from the heart.

Jesus caused the lame to walk, the deaf to hear, and the blind to see. He cleansed the poor lepers and healed all kinds of diseases.

His word drove even devils away from those whom they had been controlling. Astonished, people said, "What a word this is! For with authority and power He commands the unclean spirits, and they come out" (Luke 4:36).

At the command of Jesus, Peter was able to walk on the water. But he had to keep his eyes on the Savior. As soon as he looked away, he began to doubt and sink.

Then he cried, "Lord, save me!" (Matthew 14:30). The Savior stretched out His hand to pull Peter up out of the water. So whenever anyone cries to Him for help, Christ reaches out His hand to save.

The Savior raised the dead to life. One of them was the widow's son in the village of Nain. The people were carrying the youth to the grave when they met Jesus. He took the young man by the hand, lifted him up, and gave him alive to his mother. Then the villagers went back to their homes with shouts of rejoicing and praise to God.

Jesus also raised the daughter of Jairus. At Christ's command Lazarus, who had been dead four days, came forth from the tomb.

So when Christ shall come to earth again, His voice will pierce the tombs. "The dead in Christ will rise" to glorious immortal life and will "always be with the Lord" (1 Thessalonians 4:16, 17).

Our Lord did a wonderful work during His ministry on earth. When John the Baptist was in prison, he became despondent. He even began to wonder whether Jesus was really the Messiah. So he sent some of his followers to ask the Savior, "Are You the Coming One, or do we look for another?" (Matthew 11:3).

When the messengers reached Jesus, they found Him healing many of the sick. All day John's disciples waited while Christ worked with tireless activity to help the suffering. At last He said:

"Go and tell John the things which you hear and see: The blind see and the lame walk; the lepers are cleansed and the deaf hear; the dead are raised up and the poor have the gospel preached to them" (verses 4, 5).

So for three and a half years Jesus "went about doing good." Then the time came for His ministry on earth to end. He would go up to Jerusalem with His disciples to be betrayed, condemned, and crucified.

Thus would be fulfilled His own words: "The good shepherd gives His life for the sheep" (John 10:11). "Surely He has borne our griefs and carried our sorrows. . . . He was wounded for our transgressions, He was bruised for our iniquities; the chastisement of our peace was upon Him, and by His stripes we are healed. All we like sheep have gone astray; we have turned, every one, to his own way; and the Lord has laid on Him the iniquity of us all" (Isaiah 53:4-6).

13

Riding Into Jerusalem

Jesus was nearing Jerusalem to attend Passover. Multitudes also going up to this great yearly feast surrounded Him.

He told two of His disciples to bring a young donkey so that he might ride into the city. They spread their garments upon the animal and helped their Master get on it.

As soon as He was seated a loud shout of triumph filled the air. The crowd hailed Jesus as Messiah, their King. More than 500 years before, the prophet had foretold this scene:

"Rejoice greatly, O daughter of Zion! . . . Behold, your King is coming to you . . . lowly and riding on a donkey, a colt, the foal of a donkey" (Zechariah 9:9).

Everyone in the rapidly growing throng was happy and excited. They could not offer Him costly gifts, but they spread their outer garments as a carpet in His path.

Breaking off the beautiful branches of olive and palm trees, they scattered them across the way. They thought they were escorting Christ to take possession of the throne of David in Jerusalem.

The Savior had never before allowed His followers to show Him kingly honors. But at this time He wanted the world to recognize Him as its Redeemer.

The Son of God was about to become a sacrifice for our sins. His church in all succeeding ages would make His death a subject of deep thought and study. It was necessary, then, that everyone should now notice Him.

After such a scene nothing could ever hide His trial and crucifixion from the world. It was God's plan that each event in the closing days of the Savior's life should never be forgotten.

In the vast multitude surrounding the Savior stood people who were proof of His miracle-working power.

The blind whom He had restored to sight led the way.

Those whom He had enabled to talk again shouted the loudest praise.

The cripples whom He had healed leaped for joy. They were most active in breaking the palm branches and waving them before Him.

Widows and orphans exalted the name of Jesus for His works of mercy to them.

The loathsome lepers whom He had cleansed by a word spread their garments on the path.

Those raised from the dead by the life-giving voice of the Savior were there.

And Lazarus, whose body had begun to decay in the grave but who was now enjoying the strength of glorious health, walked with the happy throng that escorted the Savior to Jerusalem.

As new people joined the throng they caught the excitement of the hour. They added to the shouts that echoed and reechoed from hill to hill and from valley to valley:

SOJ-5

"Hosanna to the Son of David! Blessed is He who comes in the name of the Lord! Hosanna in the highest!" (Matthew 21:9).

Some of the Pharisees who watched the scene became angry. They felt that they were losing control of the people. Using all their authority, they tried to silence them, but their threats and appeals only increased the enthusiasm.

Finding that they could not control the people, they pushed their way through the crowd to where Jesus was. "Teacher, rebuke Your disciples" (Luke 19:39), they told Jesus.

They declared that such a disturbance was against the law and would not be permitted by the rulers.

Jesus said, "I tell you that if these should keep silent, the stones would immediately cry out" (verse 40).

God Himself planned this scene of triumph. The prophets had predicted it, and no earthly power could stop it. The work of God will ever go forward, in spite of all that human beings may do to hinder it or tear it down.

As the procession came to the brow of the hill overlooking Jerusalem, the full splendor of the city spread out before them.

The vast multitude hushed their shouts, spellbound by the sight. All eyes turned upon the Savior, expecting to see in His expression the same admiration they themselves felt.

Jesus halted, and a cloud of sorrow gathered upon His face. The crowd was astonished to see Him burst into tears.

Those who surrounded the Savior could not understand His grief. They did not understand that He wept for the doomed city. Anguish filled His heart as He realized that it would soon be in ruins.

Had its people listened to Christ's teaching and accepted Him as the Savior, Jerusalem would have stood forever. It might have become the world's greatest city, free in the strength of its God-given power.

There would then have been no armed soldiers waiting at her gates, no Roman banners waving from its walls.

From Jerusalem the dove of peace would have gone to all nations. The city would have been the world's crowning glory.

But the people had rejected their Savior. They were about to crucify their King. And when the sun should set that night, the doom of Jerusalem would be forever sealed. (About 40 years later the Roman army utterly destroyed and burned Jerusalem.)

By now reports had reached the local rulers that Jesus was nearing the city with a vast crowd of followers. They went out to meet Him, hoping to scatter the throng. With a show of great authority they demanded, "Who is this?" (Matthew 21:10).

The disciples, filled with the Spirit of inspiration, answered: "Adam will tell you that He is the Seed of the woman that shall bruise the serpent's head.

"Ask Abraham, and he will tell you that He is Melchizedek, King of Salem, King of peace.

"Jacob will tell you that He is Shiloh of the tribe of Judah.

"Isaiah will tell you that He is Immanuel, Wonderful, Counselor, the mighty God, the everlasting Father, the Prince of Peace.

"Jeremiah will tell you that He is the Branch of David, the Lord our righteousness.

"Daniel will tell you that He is the Messiah.

"Hosea will tell you that He is the Lord God of hosts, the Lord is His memorial.

"John the Baptist will tell you that He is the Lamb of God that takes away the sin of the world.

"The great Jehovah has proclaimed from His throne, 'This is My beloved Son.'

"We, His disciples, declare, 'This is Jesus, the Messiah, the Prince of life, the Redeemer.'

"And even the prince of the power of darkness acknowledges Him, saying, 'I know who You are—the Holy One of God!'" (Mark 1:24).

14

"Take These Things Away"

The next day Christ entered the Temple. Three years before, He had found people buying and selling in the outer court. He had rebuked them and driven them out.

Now as He came again to the Temple He found the same activity still going on. Cattle, sheep, and birds filled the courtyard. Merchants sold them to those who wished to offer sacrifice for their sins.

The merchants charged unfair prices and had other dishonest practices. So great was the noise from the stalls that it seriously disturbed the worshipers within the Temple.

Christ stood on the steps of the Temple. Again His piercing gaze swept over the courtyard. All eyes turned toward Him. The voices of the people and the noise of the cattle hushed. All looked with astonishment and awe upon the Son of God.

The divine flashed through the human and gave Jesus a dignity and glory that He had never revealed before. The silence became almost unbearable.

At last He said in clear tones and with a power that swayed the people like a mighty tempest:

"It is written, 'My house is a house of prayer,' but you have made it a 'den of thieves'" (Luke 19:46).

With still greater authority than He had shown three years before, He commanded, "Take these things away!" (John 2:16).

Once before, the priests and rulers of the Temple had fled at the sound of His voice. Afterward they were ashamed of their fear. They had decided that they would never again flee in this way.

Yet they were now more terrified and in greater haste than before to obey His command. They rushed from the Temple, driving their cattle ahead of them.

Soon the court filled with people who had brought their sick for Jesus to heal. Some were dying. The suffering people felt their great need.

They fixed their eyes imploringly upon the face of Christ, fearing to see there the severity that had driven out those who had been buying and selling the sacrificial animals. But they saw in His face only love and tender pity.

Jesus kindly received the sick. Disease and suffering fled at the touch of His hand. He tenderly gathered the children in His arms. Soothing their fretful cries, He banished sickness and pain from their little bodies. Then He handed them back, smiling and healthy, to their mothers.

What a scene greeted the priests and rulers as they cautiously made their way back to the Temple! They heard the voices of men, women, and children praising God.

The men saw the sick healed, sight restored to the blind, the deaf receive their hearing, and the lame leap for joy.

The children took the lead in the rejoicing. They repeated the hosannas of the day before and waved palm branches before the Savior. The Temple echoed and reechoed with their shouts: "Hosanna to the Son of David! 'Blessed is He who comes in the name of the Lord!'" (Matthew 21:9).

"Behold, your King is coming to you; He is just and having salvation" (Zechariah 9:9).

The rulers tried to silence the shouts of the happy children, but all were filled with joy and praise for the wonderful works of Jesus. Nothing could silence them.

The leaders then turned to the Savior, hoping that He would order everyone to be quiet. They asked Him, "Do You hear what these are saying?" (Matthew 21:16).

Jesus replied, "Yes. Have you never read, 'Out of the mouth of babes and nursing infants You have perfected praise'?" (verse 16).

The haughty rulers of the people had refused the blessed privilege of heralding the birth of Christ and forwarding His work on earth.

But someone must sound His praises, and God chose the children to do it. Had the voices of those rejoicing children been silenced, the very pillars of the Temple would have cried out in the Savior's praise.

15

At the Passover Supper

The children of Israel ate the first Passover supper at the time of their release from bondage in Egypt.

God had promised to set them free. He had told them that the firstborn son in every Egyptian family would die. Then He had told them to mark their own doorposts with the blood of a slain lamb so that the angel of death might pass them by.

The lamb itself they were to roast and eat at night, with unleavened bread and with bitter herbs. The bitter herbs represented the bitterness of their slavery.

When they ate the lamb, they must be all ready for a journey. They must have their shoes on their feet and their walking sticks in their hands.

They did as the Lord had said. That very night the king of Egypt sent them word that they might go free. In the morning they started on their way to the Land of Promise.

So every year, on the same night on which they left Egypt, all the Israelites kept the feast of the Passover at Jerusalem. At this feast each family had a roasted lamb with bread and bitter herbs, as their ancestors had had in Egypt. And they told their children the story of God's goodness in freeing His people from slavery.

The time had now come when Christ was to celebrate the feast with His disciples. He told Peter and John to find a place to meet and to prepare the Passover supper.

A great many people came to Jerusalem at this time. Those who lived in the city were always ready to offer a room in their house for visitors to keep the feast.

The Savior told Peter and John that when they had gone into the street, they would meet a man carrying a pitcher of water. They were to follow him and enter the house where he went. And they were to say to the owner of that house, "The Teacher says to you, 'Where is the guest room where I may eat the Passover with My disciples?'" (Luke 22:11). The man would then show them a large upper room furnished for their needs. There they were to prepare the Passover supper. And it

all happened just as the Savior had told them it would.

At the Passover supper the disciples were alone with Jesus. The times they spent with Him at such feasts had always been occasions of joy, but now He seemed troubled.

At last He said to them sadly, "With fervent desire I have desired to eat this Passover with you before I suffer" (verse 15).

Picking up a cup of wine, He gave thanks and said, "Take this and divide it among yourselves; for I say to you, I will not drink of the fruit of the vine until the kingdom of God comes" (verses 17, 18).

It was the last time that Christ would celebrate the feast with His disciples. Also it was really the last Passover that was ever to be kept. The lamb had been slain to teach the people about Christ's death. When Christ, the Lamb of God, should be slain for the sins of the world, there would no longer be any need to sacrifice a lamb to represent His death.

When the Jewish leaders put Christ to death, they rejected all that gave to this feast its value and significance.

As Christ joined in the Passover service He thought of His last great sacrifice. He was now in the shadow of the cross, and the pain of it tortured His heart. Our Savior knew all the anguish that awaited Him.

Jesus knew the ingratitude and cruelty that would be shown Him by those He had come to save. But it was not about His own suffering that He thought. Instead, He pitied those who would reject their Savior and lose eternal life.

And the thought of His disciples was uppermost in His mind. He knew that after His own suffering was over, they would be left to struggle in the world.

Jesus wanted to tell them many things that would comfort their hearts when He should walk no more with them. He had hoped to speak about these things at their last meeting before His death.

But He could not tell them now. Christ saw that they were not ready to listen.

The disciples had been arguing among themselves. They still thought that Christ would soon become King. Each of them wanted the highest place in His kingdom. So they had jealous and angry feelings toward one another.

There was still another cause of trouble. At a feast it was the custom for a servant to wash the feet of the guests. The pitcher of water, the basin, and the towel were there, ready for the foot-washing. But no servant was present, and it was the disciples' part to perform it.

But each disciple refused to be a servant to the rest. He was not willing to wash their feet. So in silence they had taken their places at the table.

Jesus waited a while to see what they would do. Then He Himself rose from the table. He wrapped the towel around Himself, poured water into the basin, and began to wash the disciples' feet. Although their struggle to be first hurt Him deeply, He did not scold them. He showed His love by acting as a servant to His own disciples.

When He had finished, He said to them:

"If I then, your Lord and Teacher, have washed your feet, you also ought to wash one another's feet. For I have given you an example, that you should do as I have done to you" (John 13:14, 15).

In this way Christ taught them that they ought to help one another. Instead of seeking the highest place, each should be willing to serve the others.

The Savior came into the world to work for others. Jesus lived to help and save the needy and sinful. He wants us to do as He did.

The disciples were ashamed of their jealousy and selfishness. Love for their Lord and for one another filled their hearts. Now they could pay attention to Christ's teaching.

As they still sat at the table Jesus took bread, said a prayer of thanks, tore it into pieces, and passed it out to them. "This is My body which is given for you; do this in remembrance of Me," He said (Luke 22:19).

Then after the meal He took the cup and said, "This cup is the new covenant in My blood, which is shed for you" (verse 20).

The Bible says: "For as often as you eat this bread and drink this cup, you proclaim the Lord's death till He comes" (1 Corinthians 11:26).

The bread and the wine represent the body and the blood of Christ. As the bread was broken and the wine was poured out, so on the cross Christ's body was broken and His blood was shed to save us.

By eating the bread and drinking the wine, we show that we believe this. We indicate that we repent of our sins and that we accept Christ as our Savior.

As the disciples sat at the table with Jesus they saw that He still seemed greatly troubled. A cloud of gloom settled on them all, and they ate in silence.

At last Jesus spoke and said, "Assuredly, I say to you, one of you will betray Me" (Matthew 26:21).

His words hurt and amazed His disciples. Each began to look into his heart to see if it had any shadow of an evil thought against their Master.

One after another they asked, "Lord, is it I?" (verse 22).

Judas alone remained silent. His silence caught everyone's attention. When he saw that the others noticed that he hadn't said anything, he too asked, "Rabbi, is it I?" (verse 25).

And Jesus solemnly replied, "You have said it" (verse 25).

Jesus had washed the feet of Judas, but this had not caused him to love the Savior more. It made him angry that Christ should do a servant's work. Now he knew that Christ would not become king. He was more determined than ever to betray Him.

Even when he saw that Christ knew his purpose, it did not change his mind. In anger he quickly left the room to carry out his wicked plan.

Everyone felt a sense of relief when Judas departed. The Savior's face relaxed, and the shadow of sadness lifted from the disciples.

Christ now talked for some time with His disciples. He was going to His Father's house, He said, to prepare a place for them. Then He would return to take them home with Him.

Jesus promised to send the Holy Spirit to be their teacher and comforter while He was gone. If they would pray in His name, their prayers would surely be answered.

Then He prayed for them. Christ asked the Father to protect them from evil to help them love one another as He had loved them.

Jesus prayed for us as well as for the first disciples. He said:

"I do not pray for these alone, but also for those who will believe in Me through their word; that they all may be one, as You, Father, are in Me, and I in You; that they may also be one in Us, that the world may believe that You sent Me. . . . and have loved them as You have loved Me" (John 17:20-23).

16

In Gethsemane

The Savior's life on earth was one of constant prayer. He spent many hours alone with God and often made earnest petitions to His heavenly Father. Thus He received strength and wisdom to sustain Him in His work and to keep Him from falling under the temptations of Satan.

After eating the Passover supper with His disciples, Jesus went with them to the garden of Gethsemane. There He often spent time in prayer. As they walked along He talked with them and taught them. But when they neared the garden, He became strangely silent.

All His life Jesus had lived in the presence of His Father. The Spirit of God had been His constant guide and support. He always gave God the glory for His works on earth and said, "I can of Myself do nothing" (John 5:30).

We can do nothing by ourselves. It is only by relying on Christ for all our strength that we can overcome sin and temptation and do His will on earth. We must have the same simple, childlike trust in Jesus that He had in His Father. Christ said: "Without Me you can do nothing" (John 15:5).

The terrible night of agony for the Savior began as they neared the garden. It seemed that God's presence, which had been His constant support, was no longer with Him. He was beginning to feel what it was to be shut out from His Father.

Christ must bear the sins of the world. As they were now laid upon Him, they seemed more than He could endure. The sense of the guilt of sin was so terrible that He was tempted to fear that God could no longer love Him.

As the terrible displeasure of the Father against evil overwhelmed Him, the words were forced from Him: "My soul is exceedingly sorrowful, even to death" (Matthew 26:38).

Jesus had left all His disciples near the gate of Gethsemane except for Peter, James, and John. They went into the garden with Him. The three of them were His most earnest followers and had been His closest companions. But He could not bear that even they should witness the suffering He was to endure. "Stay here and watch with Me" (verse 38), He said to them.

Christ went a short distance away and collapsed upon the ground. He felt sin separating Him from the Father. The gulf between Them appeared so broad, so black, so deep, that He shuddered before it.

Our Savior was suffering not for His own sins, but for those of the world. He was feeling God's displeasure against sin as sinners will feel it in the great judgment day.

In His agony Christ clung to the cold ground. From His pale lips came the bitter cry, "O My Father, if it is possible, let this cup pass from Me; nevertheless, not as I will, but as You will" (verse 39).

For an hour Christ endured this terrible suffering alone. Then He returned to the disciples, hoping for some word of sympathy. But they were asleep. They awoke at the sound of His voice, but they hardly recognized Him. His anguish had greatly changed His face. Turning to Peter, He said, "Simon, are you sleeping? Could you not watch one hour?" (Mark 14:37).

Just before Jesus and all the disciples had reached Gethsemane, Christ had said to them, "All of you will be made to stumble because of Me this night" (Mark 14:27). They had assured Him that they would go with Him even to prison and to death. And poor self-sufficient Peter had added, "Even if all are made to stumble, yet I will not be" (verse 29).

But the disciples trusted in themselves. They did not look to the Mighty Helper as Christ had counseled them to do. So when the Savior most needed their sympathy and prayers, He found them asleep. Even Peter was sleeping.

And John, the loving disciple who had leaned upon the breast of Jesus, was also asleep. Surely John's love for his Master should have kept him awake. His earnest prayers should have mingled with those of his loved Savior in the time of His great agony. The Redeemer had spent whole nights in praying for His disciples, that their faith might not fail in the hour of trial. Yet they could not remain awake with Him even one hour.

Had Christ now asked James and John, "Are you able to drink the cup that I drink, and be baptized with the baptism that I am baptized

with?" (Mark 10:38), they would not have answered so readily as they did before, "We are able" (verse 39).

Pity and sympathy at the weakness of His disciples filled the Savior's heart. He feared that they could not endure the test that His suffering and death would bring upon them.

Yet He did not scold them for their weakness. He thought of the trials ahead of them. "Watch and pray, lest you enter into temptation" (Matthew 26:41), He said.

He made an excuse for their failure in their duty toward Him: "The spirit indeed is willing, but the flesh is weak" (verse 41). What an example of the Savior's tender, loving concern!

Again superhuman agony seized the Son of God. Fainting and exhausted, He staggered back into the garden and again prayed, "O My Father, if this cup cannot pass away from Me unless I drink it, Your will be done" (verse 42).

The agony of His prayer forced drops of blood from His pores. Again He sought the disciples for sympathy, and again He found them sleeping. But they woke up as He approached. They stared at His face with fear, for blood covered it. They could not understand the mental anguish that His face revealed.

A third time He sought the place of prayer. A dark horror overcame Him. He had lost the presence of His Father. Without this, He feared that in His human nature He could not endure the test.

The third time He prayed the same prayer as before. Angels longed to help Him, but they could not rush to His aid. The Son of God must drink this cup, or the world would be lost forever. As He struggled there He saw humanity's helplessness. He saw the power of sin over people. The woes of a doomed world passed in review before Him.

At last He made the final decision. He would save the human race no matter what the cost to Himself. Jesus had left the courts of heaven, where all is purity, happiness, and glory, to save the one lost sheep, the one fallen world. Nothing would stop Him from His purpose. His prayer now revealed only submission to the divine plan:

"If this cup cannot pass away from Me unless I drink it, Your will be done."

The Savior now fell dying to the ground. No disciple was there to place his hand tenderly beneath his Master's head and bathe that brow. Christ was alone.

But God suffered with His Son. Angels beheld the Savior's agony. Heaven watched in hushed silence. Could humanity have viewed the amazement of the angelic host as in silent grief they watched the Father separating His beams of light, love, and glory from His beloved Son, it would better understand how offensive sin is in His sight.

A mighty angel now came to Christ's side. He lifted the head of the divine sufferer against his chest and pointed toward heaven. The angel told Him that He had won against Satan. As the result, millions will be victors in His glorious kingdom.

A heavenly peace rested upon the Savior's bloodstained face. He had borne that which no human being can ever bear. Jesus had tasted the sufferings of death for every person.

Again Christ sought His disciples, and again He discovered them sleeping. Had they remained awake, watching and praying with their Savior, they would have received help for the trial before them. But because they had slept, they had no strength in their hour of need.

Looking sadly at them, Christ said, "Are you still sleeping and resting? Behold, the hour is at hand, and the Son of Man is being betrayed into the hands of sinners" (verse 45).

Even as He spoke He heard the footsteps of the mob in search of Him. "Rise, let us be going," He said. "See, My betrayer is at hand" (verse 46).

17

The Betrayal and Arrest

The Savior showed no traces of His recent suffering as He stepped forth to meet His betrayer. Standing ahead of His disciples, He asked the mob, "Whom are you seeking?" (John 18:4).

They answered, "Jesus of Nazareth" (verse 5).

Jesus replied, "I am He" (verse 5).

As Jesus spoke these words the angel who had recently come to help Him moved between Him and the mob. A divine light illuminated the Savior's face, and a dovelike form overshadowed Him.

The divine glory overwhelmed the murderous throng. They staggered backward. The priests, elders, and soldiers dropped to the ground.

Then the angel withdrew, and the light faded away. Jesus could have escaped, but He remained, calm and self-possessed. His disciples were too amazed to say a word.

The Roman soldiers soon got to their feet. Along with the priests and Judas, they gathered about Christ. They seemed ashamed of their weakness, and fearful that He would escape. Again the Redeemer asked, "Whom are you seeking?" (verse 7).

Again they answered, "Jesus of Nazareth."

The Savior then said, "I have told you that I am He. Therefore, if you seek Me, let these [pointing to His disciples] go their way" (verse 8).

Even in His hour of trial Christ was concerned about His beloved disciples. He did not wish to have them suffer, even though He must go to prison and to death.

Judas, the betrayer, approached Jesus and kissed Him.

Jesus said to him, "Friend, why have you come?" (Matthew 26:50). His voice trembled as He added, "Judas, are you betraying the Son of Man with a kiss?" (Luke 22:48).

The gentle words should have touched the heart of Judas. But all tenderness and honor seemed to have left him. Judas had yielded himself to Satan's control. He stood boldly before the Lord and was not ashamed to give Him up to the cruel mob.

Christ did not refuse the traitor's kiss. By accepting it He gave us an example of love and concern for others. If we are His disciples, we must treat our enemies as He treated Judas.

The murderous throng became bold as they saw Judas touch the person they had so recently seen blazing with glory. They seized the Savior and bound those hands that had been constantly doing good.

The disciples did not think that Christ would allow Himself to be taken. They knew that the power that had already stunned the mob could keep them helpless till Christ and they could escape.

But to their great disappointment and anger they saw ropes tied around the hands of the Jesus they loved. Peter, in his anger, rashly drew his sword and tried to defend his Master. But he only cut off an ear of the high priest's servant.

When Jesus saw what had happened, He released His hands, though held firmly by the Roman soldiers. "Permit even this," He said (Luke 22:51). Then He touched the wounded ear, and it was instantly made whole.

Then He ordered Peter, "Put your sword in its place, for all who take the sword will perish by the sword. Or do you think that I cannot now pray to My Father, and He will provide Me with more than twelve legions of angels? How then could the Scriptures be fulfilled, that it must happen thus?" (Matthew 26:52-54). "Shall I not drink the cup which My Father has given Me?" (John 18:11).

Christ then turned to the chief priests and the Temple police, who were with the mob, and said, "Have you come out, as against a robber, with swords and clubs to take Me? I was daily with you in the temple teaching, and you did not seize Me. But the Scriptures must be fulfilled" (Mark 14:48, 49).

It upset the disciples when they saw that the Savior made no effort to escape His enemies. They blamed Him for not doing so and could not understand why He submitted to the mob. Terror-stricken, His followers fled.

Christ had already predicted their desertion. "Indeed," He had said, "the hour is coming, yes, has now come, that you will be scattered, each to his own, and will leave Me alone. And yet I am not alone, because the Father is with Me" (John 16:32).

18

Before Annas, Caiaphas, and the Sanhedrin

The shouting mob followed Jesus from Gethsemane. He moved painfully, for His hands were tightly bound, and He was closely guarded.

The mob first dragged Him to the house of Annas, who had formerly been the high priest, but whose place then had been filled by his son-in-law, Caiaphas. The wicked Annas had requested that he might be the first to see Jesus of Nazareth a bound captive. He hoped to draw from Him some evidence to condemn Him by.

With this in mind he questioned the Savior about His disciples and His teachings. Christ answered:

"I spoke openly to the world. I always taught in synagogues and in the temple, where the Jews always meet, and in secret I have said nothing" (John 18:20).

Then, facing His questioner, He said, "Why do you ask Me? Ask those who have heard Me what I said to them" (verse 21).

The priests themselves had sent spies to watch Christ and report His every word. Through their agents they knew His teachings and actions at every gathering He had attended. The spies had sought to entrap Him in His words, that they might find something by which to condemn Him. So the Savior said, "Ask those who heard Me. Go to your spies. They have heard what I have said. They can tell you what My teaching has been."

Christ's words were so searching and pointed that the priest felt that his prisoner was reading his very soul.

But one of the servants of Annas, thinking that Jesus did not treat his master with proper respect, struck Christ in the face, blurting out, "Do You answer the high priest like that?" (verse 22).

To this Jesus mildly said, "If I have spoken evil, bear witness of the evil; but if well, why do you strike Me?" (verse 23).

Christ could have summoned legions of angels from heaven to His aid. But it was a part of His mission to endure in His humanity all the taunts and insults that people might heap upon Him.

The Temple authorities took the Savior from the house of Annas to the palace of Caiaphas. They would try Him before the Sanhedrin. Annas and Caiaphas again questioned Him while they had its members called together, but they learned nothing new from Jesus.

When the members of the Sanhedrin had assembled, Caiaphas took his seat as president. On each side were the judges. In front of them stood the Roman soldiers guarding the Savior. Behind the soldiers was the accusing mob.

Caiaphas then ordered Jesus to do one of His mighty miracles before them. But the Savior gave no sign that He had heard a word. Had He responded by even one soul-searching look, such as He gave the buyers and sellers in the Temple, the whole murderous throng would have had to flee from His presence.

The Romans controlled Palestine and did not allow the Jews to punish anyone with death. The Sanhedrin could only examine the prisoner and pass along its judgment to the Roman authorities. The Romans would then decide whether to execute the prisoner or not.

To get Christ killed, they must find something against the Savior that the Roman governor would regard as a crime. They had lots of evidence that Christ had spoken against the Jewish traditions and many of their rules. It was easy to prove that He had denounced the priests and scribes and that He had called them hypocrites and murderers. But the Romans would pay no attention to that, for they themselves were disgusted with the Pharisees.

Many charges were brought against Christ, but either the witnesses disagreed, or the evidence was of such a nature that the Romans would not accept it. The religious leaders tried to make Him reply to their accusations, but He appeared as if He had not heard them.

Long before, the prophet Isaiah had described Christ's silence at this time:

"He was oppressed and He was afflicted, yet He opened not His mouth; He was led as a lamb to the slaughter, and as a sheep before its shearers is silent, so He opened not His mouth" (Isaiah 53:7).

The priests began to fear that they would not find any evidence to use against their prisoner before Pilate. They felt that they must make one last effort. The high priest raised his right hand toward heaven and said to Jesus, "I put You under oath by the living God: Tell us if You are the Christ, the Son of God!" (Matthew 26:63).

The Savior never denied His mission or His relationship to the Father. He could remain silent to personal insult. But He always spoke plainly and decidedly when anyone questioned His work or Sonship to God.

Every ear listened carefully, and every eye was fixed upon Him as He answered, "It is as you said" (verse 64).

In the custom of those days what Jesus said was the same as answering yes. It was the strongest way one could make an affirmative answer. A heavenly light seemed to illuminate the pale face of the Savior as He added, "Nevertheless, I say to you, hereafter you will see the Son of Man sitting at the right hand of the Power, and coming on the clouds of heaven" (verse 64).

In His statement the Savior presented the reverse of what was then taking place. He pointed forward to the time when He would occupy the position of supreme judge of heaven and earth. Christ will then be seated upon the Father's throne, and His decisions will have no appeal.

He brought before His listeners a view of that day, when, instead of being surrounded and abused by a riotous mob, He would come in the clouds of heaven with power and great glory. Legions of angels would escort Him. Then He would pronounce sentence upon His enemies, including that same accusing throng.

As Jesus spoke the words declaring Himself to be the Son of God and judge of the world, the high priest rent his robe, as if to show his horror. He lifted his hands toward heaven and said, "He has spoken blasphemy! What further need do we have of witnesses? Look, now you have heard His blasphemy! What do you think?" (verses 65, 66).

The judges answered, "He is deserving of death" (verse 66).

It was contrary to the Jewish law to try a prisoner at night. Though they had condemned Christ, they must still conduct a formal trial during the day.

The authorities took Jesus to the guard room. There He endured mockery and abuse from the soldiers and the crowd.

At daybreak the guards again brought Him before His judges, who pronounced the final sentence.

A satanic fury then took possession of the leaders and the people. The roar of voices was like that of wild beasts. They rushed toward Jesus, screaming, "He is guilty; put Him to death!" Had it not been for the soldiers, they would have torn Him in pieces. The Romans used their weapons to keep the mob back.

Priests, rulers, and the rabble joined in abusing the Savior. Someone threw an old garment over His head, and His persecutors struck Him in the face. "Prophesy to us, Christ! Who is the one who struck You?" (verse 68).

When the garment was removed, one of the mocking throng spat in the Savior's face.

The angels of God faithfully recorded every insulting look, word, and act against their beloved Commander. One day those who scorned and spat upon the calm, pale face of Christ will see it shining brighter than the sun.

19

Judas

The Jewish rulers had been eager to get Jesus into their power, but because of their fear of triggering a riot among the people, they had not dared to seize Him openly. So they had sought someone who would secretly betray Him. In Judas, one of the 12 disciples, they found the man who would do this terrible thing.

Judas had a strong desire for money, but he had not always been wicked and corrupt enough to do such a deed. He had let greed rule his life until he could now sell his Lord for 30 pieces of silver, the price of a slave (Exodus 21:28-32). He could now betray the Savior with a kiss in Gethsemane.

But he continued to follow every step of the Son of God as He went from Gethsemane to the trial before the Jewish rulers. He did not really believe that the Savior would allow the religious leaders to kill Him, as they had threatened to do.

At any moment Judas expected to see Him released and protected by divine power, as had happened in the past. But as the hours went by and Jesus quietly submitted to all the indignities heaped upon Him, a terrible fear crept into the traitor's mind. He began to believe that he had indeed betrayed his Master to His death.

As the trial drew to a close Judas could endure the torture of his guilty conscience no longer. All at once his hoarse voice rang through the hall. It frightened all those who heard it.

"He is innocent. Spare Him, O Caiaphas. He has done nothing worthy of death!"

The startled crowd saw the tall Judas pushing his way through its midst. His face was pale and haggard, and large drops of sweat stood on his forehead. Rushing to the throne of judgment, he threw down before the high priest the pieces of silver that had been the price of his Lord's betrayal.

Grasping the robe of Caiaphas, he begged him to release Jesus, declaring that He had done no wrong. Angrily Caiaphas shook him off and said with scorn, "What is that to us? You see to it" (Matthew 27:4).

Judas then threw himself at the Savior's feet. He confessed that Jesus was the Son of God, and begged Him to deliver Himself from His enemies.

The Savior knew that Judas did not really repent for what he had done. The false disciple feared that punishment would come upon him for his terrible deed. He felt no real sorrow that he had betrayed the spotless Son of God.

Yet Christ spoke no word of condemnation to him. He looked with pity upon Judas and said, "For this hour I came into the world."

A murmur of surprise ran through the assembly. With amazement they beheld the forbearance of Christ toward His betrayer.

Judas saw that his pleading was in vain. He rushed from the hall, crying, "It is too late! It is too late!"

The betrayer felt that He could not bear to see Jesus crucified. In despair he went out and hanged himself.

Later that same day, on the road from Pilate's judgment hall to Calvary, the wicked throng were leading the Savior to the place of crucifixion. Suddenly their shouts and jeers stopped. As they passed a secluded spot they saw at the foot of a lifeless tree the dead body of Judas.

It was a revolting sight. His weight had broken the rope he had used to hang himself. The fall had horribly mangled his body. Wild dogs were now devouring it.

His remains were immediately buried out of sight. But people did not mock as much, and many a pale face revealed the fearful thoughts within. Retribution seemed already to be visiting those who were guilty of the blood of Jesus.

20

Before Pilate

After the Sanhedrin had condemned Christ, the religious leaders took Him at once to Pilate, the Roman governor, to have the sentence confirmed and executed.

The Jewish priests and rulers could not enter Pilate's judgment hall themselves. According to the ceremonial laws of their nation, they would defile themselves if they did so. It would prevent them from taking part in the feast of the Passover.

In their spiritual blindness they did not see that Christ was the real Passover lamb. Since they had rejected Him, the great feast had for them lost its meaning.

As Pilate beheld Jesus he saw a noble and dignified man. Christ's face showed no trace of evil. Pilate turned to the priests and asked, "What accusation do you bring against this Man?" (John 18:29).

His enemies were not prepared for the question. They knew that they could bring no truthful evidence on which the Roman governor would condemn Him. So the priests called the false witnesses to their aid. "And they began to accuse Him, saying, 'We found this fellow perverting the nation, and forbidding to pay taxes to Caesar, saying that He Himself is Christ, a King'" (Luke 23:2).

This was false, for Christ had plainly permitted the payment of taxes to Caesar. When the religious leaders had tried to entrap Him on this very matter, He had said, "Render therefore to Caesar the things that are Caesar's" (Matthew 22:21).

The testimony of the false witnesses did not fool Pilate. He turned to the Savior and asked, "'Are You the King of the Jews?' Jesus said to him, 'It is as you say'" (Matthew 27:11).

When they heard this answer, Caiaphas and those who were with him called Pilate to witness that Jesus had admitted the crime of which they accused Him. Noisily they demanded that Pilate sentence Him to death.

When Christ did not answer His accusers, Pilate said to Him, "'Do You answer nothing? See how many things they testify against You!'

"But Jesus still answered nothing" (Mark 15:4, 5).

Pilate was perplexed. He saw no evidence of crime in Jesus, and he had no confidence in those accusing Him. The noble appearance and quiet manner of the Savior contrasted with the excitement and fury of the religious leaders. Impressed with this, the Roman official was satisfied that He was innocent.

Hoping to gain the truth from Him, he took Jesus off by Himself. "Are You the King of the Jews?" (John 18:33) he questioned.

Christ did not give a direct answer, but instead asked, "Are you speaking for yourself about this, or did others tell you this concerning Me?" (verse 34).

The Spirit of God was working on Pilate. Jesus wanted His question to lead him to examine his own heart more closely. Pilate understood the meaning of the question. As his own heart opened before him, he felt convicted. But pride arose in his heart.

"Am I a Jew? Your own nation and the chief priests have delivered You to me.

What have You done?" (verse 35).

Pilate's golden opportunity had passed. But Jesus desired Pilate to understand that He had not come to be an earthly king. "My kingdom is not of this world. If My kingdom were of this world, My servants would fight, so that I should not be delivered to the Jews; but now My kingdom is not from here" (verse 36).

Pilate then asked, "'Are You a king then?'

"Jesus answered, 'You say rightly that I am a king. For this cause I was born, and for this cause I have come into the world, that I should bear witness to the truth. Everyone who is of the truth hears My voice'" (verse 37).

Pilate had a desire to know the truth. His mind was confused. He eagerly grasped the words of the Savior. As his heart stirred with a great longing to know what the truth really was and how he could obtain it, he asked Jesus, "What is truth?" (verse 38).

But he did not wait to receive an answer. The tumult of the crowd outside the hall of justice had increased to a roar. The priests clamored for immediate action. Their shouts reminded Pilate that he must make a decision. Going out to the people, he declared, "I find no fault in Him at all" (verse 38).

These words from a pagan judge were a scathing rebuke to the falsehood of the rulers of Israel who were accusing the Savior.

As the priests and elders heard Pilate's conclusion their disappointment and rage exploded. They had long plotted and waited for this opportunity. As they saw the possibility that Pilate might release Jesus they seemed ready to tear Him in pieces.

They lost all reason and self-control. Cursing and denouncing Pilate, they behaved more like demons than human beings. The rulers threatened to get him into trouble with the Roman government. They accused Pilate of refusing to condemn Jesus, who, they claimed, had set Himself up against Caesar. Then they shouted, "He stirs up the people, teaching throughout all Judea, beginning from Galilee to this place" (Luke 23:5).

Pilate at this time had no thought of condemning Jesus. He was sure of His innocence. But when he heard that Christ was from Galilee, he decided to send Him to Herod, the ruler of that province, who was then in Jerusalem. By doing this, Pilate tried to shift the responsibility of the trial from himself to Herod.

Jesus was faint from hunger and weary from loss of sleep. He was also suffering from the cruel treatment He had received. But Pilate again turned Him over to the soldiers. The soldiers dragged Him away amid the jeers and insults of the merciless mob.

21

Before Herod

Although Herod had never met Jesus, he had long desired to see Him. He hoped that Jesus would display His marvelous power. As the soldiers brought the Savior before him, the rabble surged and pressed about, shouting all kinds of things. Herod commanded silence, for he wished to question the prisoner.

He looked with curiosity and pity upon the pale face of Christ. The ruler of Galilee saw there the marks of deep wisdom and purity. Herod concluded, as Pilate already had, that malice and envy alone had caused the religious leaders to accuse the Savior.

Now Herod urged Christ to perform one of His wonderful miracles before him. He promised to release Him if He would do so. At his orders crippled and deformed persons were brought in. Then Herod commanded Jesus to heal them. But the Savior stood before Herod as if He neither saw nor heard anything.

The Son of God had taken upon Himself humanity's nature. He must do as a human being must do in similar circumstances. Therefore He would not work a miracle to gratify curiosity or to save Himself from the kind of pain and humiliation that we must endure when placed in a similar position.

It terrified Jesus' accusers when Herod demanded a miracle. Above everything else they dreaded most that He might exhibit His divine power. A miracle would destroy their plans and would perhaps cost them their lives. So they shouted that Jesus worked miracles through the power given Him by Beelzebub, the prince of the devils.

Several years earlier Herod had listened to the teaching of John the Baptist. What John had said had deeply impressed the ruler, but he would not give up his life of sin. So his heart grew harder. At last, while drunk, he had commanded that John should be slain to please the wicked Herodias.

Now he had become still more hardened. He could not bear the silence of

Jesus. His face grew dark with anger, and he angrily threatened Jesus. But the Savior remained unmoved and silent.

Christ had come into the world to heal the brokenhearted. If He could have said anything that would have helped someone, He would not have kept silent. But He had no words for those who trampled the truth under their unholy feet.

The Savior might have spoken to Herod words that would have grabbed the attention of the hardened king. He might have stricken him with fear and trembling by laying before him the full iniquity of his life and the horror of his approaching doom. But Christ's silence was the severest rebuke that He could have given.

That ear that had always been open to the cry of human woe now had no place for the command of Herod. That heart, ever touched by the plea of even the worst sinners, was closed to the haughty king who felt no need of a Savior.

Angry, Herod turned to the crowd and denounced Jesus as an impostor. But the Savior's accusers knew that He was no impostor. They had seen too many of His mighty works not to believe.

Then the king began to shamefully abuse and ridicule the Son of God. "Herod, with his men of war, treated Him with contempt and mocked Him, arrayed Him in a gorgeous robe, and sent Him back to Pilate" (Luke 23:11).

As the wicked king saw Jesus accepting all this indignity in silence, he felt a sudden fear that this was no ordinary person in front of him. The thought that this prisoner might be a heavenly being come down to earth frightened him.

Herod did not dare to approve the charge against Jesus. Wishing to escape the terrible responsibility, he sent the Savior back to the Roman governor.

22

Condemned by Pilate

When the Jewish leaders returned from Herod, bringing the Savior again to Pilate, the Roman official was greatly displeased. First he asked what they wanted him to do. Then he reminded them that he had examined Jesus and had found no fault in Him. He told them that while they had brought complaints against Him, they had not been able to prove a single charge.

Furthermore, they had taken Him to Herod, who was a Jew like themselves, and he had found in Him nothing worthy of death. But to pacify the accusers, Pilate said, "I will therefore chastise Him and release Him" (Luke 23:16).

Here Pilate showed his weakness. He had acknowledged that Christ was innocent. Why then should he punish Him? It was a compromise with wrong. The religious leaders never forgot this all during Jesus' trial. They had intimidated the Roman governor.

Now they would use their advantage until they secured the condemnation of Jesus.

The crowd clamored even more loudly for the death of the prisoner.

While Pilate hesitated as to what he should do, a letter came from his wife. It told him:

"Have nothing to do with that just Man, for I have suffered many things today in a dream because of Him" (Matthew 27:19).

Pilate turned pale at this message. But the mob became more demanding as they saw his indecision.

The Roman official saw that he had to do something. It was customary at the feast of the Passover to set free one prisoner whom the people might choose. The Roman soldiers had recently captured a notorious robber named Barabbas. He was a murderer. Pilate turned to the crowd, and said with great earnestness:

"Whom do you want me to release to you? Barabbas, or Jesus who is called Christ?" (verse 17).

They replied, "Away with this Man, and release to us Barabbas" (Luke 23:18).

Pilate was speechless with surprise and disappointment. By appealing to the people, he had lost his dignity and the control of the crowd. After that, he was only the mob's tool. They swayed him at their will. "What then shall I do with Jesus who is called Christ?" he asked (Matthew 27:22).

With one voice they cried, "'Let Him be crucified!'

"Then the governor said, 'Why, what evil has He done?'

"But they cried out all the more, saying, 'Let Him be crucified!'" (verses 22, 23).

Pilate's cheeks paled as he heard the terrible cry, "Let Him be crucified." He had not thought it would come to that. Repeatedly he had declared Jesus innocent. But the people were determined that He should suffer this most terrible and dreaded death. Again the Roman governor asked, "Why, what evil has He done?"

And again the mob shouted, "Crucify Him, crucify Him!"

Pilate made one last effort to touch their sympathy. He had Jesus, faint with weariness and covered with wounds, scourged in their sight.

"And the soldiers twisted a crown of thorns and put it on His head, and they put on Him a purple robe. Then they said, 'Hail, King of the Jews!' And they struck Him with their hands" (John 19:2, 3).

They spit upon Him. Someone snatched the reed that the soldiers had placed in His hand and hit the crown upon His brow, forcing the thorns into His temples. Blood trickled down His face and beard.

Satan led the cruel soldiers in their abuse of the Savior. He hoped to provoke Jesus into retaliating, if possible, or to drive Him to perform a miracle to release Himself. That would destroy the plan of salvation. One stain upon His human life, one failure of His humanity to bear the terrible test, and the Lamb of God would have been an imperfect offering. His redemption of the human race would have been a failure.

He, the commander of the heavenly host, could have instantly called to His aid legions of holy angels. Just one of those angels could have immediately overpowered that cruel mob. Jesus could have stricken down His tormentors by flashing forth His divine majesty. But instead He submitted with dignity to the coarsest insult and outrage.

As the acts of His torturers degraded them below the level of humanity—into the likeness of Satan—so did Jesus' meekness and patience exalt Him above humanity. It proved His kinship to God.

The uncomplaining patience of the Savior deeply moved Pilate. He had Barabbas brought into the court. Then he presented the two prisoners side by side. Pointing to the Savior, he said in a voice of solemn entreaty, "Behold the Man!" (John 19:5). "I am bringing Him out to you, that you may know that I find no fault in Him" (verse 4).

There stood the Son of God, wearing the robe of mockery and the crown of thorns. Stripped to the waist, His back showed long, cruel, bleeding wounds. His blood-covered face showed His exhaustion and pain. But never had it appeared more beautiful. Every feature expressed gentleness and resignation and the tenderest concern for His cruel foes.

In striking contrast was the prisoner at His side. Every line in the face of Barabbas showed him to be the hardened criminal that he was.

Some in the crowd sympathized with Jesus. Even the priests and rulers were convicted that He was what He claimed to be. But they would not yield. They had moved the mob to a mad fury, and again priests, rulers, and people raised the cry, "Crucify Him, crucify Him!" (verse 6).

At last, losing all patience with their unreasonable, vengeful cruelty, Pilate said to them, "You take Him and crucify Him, for I find no fault in Him" (verse 6).

Pilate tried hard to free the Savior; but the mob shouted, "If you let this Man go, you are not Caesar's friend. Whoever makes himself a king speaks against Caesar" (John 19:12).

This touched Pilate in a weak spot. He was already under suspicion by the Roman government. A report of this kind would ruin him.

"When Pilate saw that he could not prevail at all, but rather that a tumult was rising, he took water and washed his hands before the multitude, saying, 'I am innocent of the blood of this just Person. You see to it'" (Matthew 27:24).

In vain Pilate tried to free himself from the guilt of condemning Jesus. Had he acted promptly and firmly at the first, carrying out his convictions of right, the mob would not have overcome him. They would not have dared to dictate to him.

His wavering and indecision proved his ruin. He saw that he could not release Jesus and still retain his own position and influence.

Rather than lose his worldly power, he chose to sacrifice an innocent life. Yielding to the demands of the mob, he again scourged Jesus. Then he turned Him over to the soldiers to be crucified.

But in spite of his precautions, the very thing that he dreaded still happened. His honors were stripped from him and he was cast down from his high office. Stung by remorse and wounded pride, he ended his own life.

So all who compromise with sin will gain only sorrow and ruin. "There is a way that seems right to a man, but its end is the way of death" (Prov. 14:12).

When Pilate declared himself innocent of the blood of Christ, Caiaphas answered defiantly, "His blood be on us and on our children" (Matthew 27:25).

The priests echoed the terrible words, and the mob reechoed them.

It was a terrible sentence to pass upon themselves. The destruction of Jerusalem about 40 years later literally fulfilled it. Doubly literal will be the fulfillment when "this same Jesus" will come (Acts 1:11) and "in flaming fire taking vengeance on those who do not know God" (2 Thessalonians 1:8).

Then they will pray to the rocks and mountains:

"Fall on us and hide us from the face of Him who sits on the throne and from the wrath of the Lamb! For the great day of His wrath has come" (Revelation 6:16, 17).

23

Calvary

The soldiers hurried Jesus to Calvary amid the shouts and jeers of the crowd. As He passed the gate of Pilate's court, a soldier lay the heavy cross prepared for Barabbas upon Christ's bruised and bleeding shoulders. Other soldiers placed crosses upon two thieves, who were to die with Jesus.

The load was too heavy for the Savior in His exhausted condition. He had gone but a short distance when He fainted under the weight of the cross.

When He revived, His guards again placed the cross upon His shoulders. He staggered on a few steps and once again fell to the ground. The soldiers now realized that it was impossible for Him to go farther with His burden. They wondered where they could find someone who would carry the humiliating load.

Just then Simon, a Cyrenian, met them as he came from the opposite direction.

The Romans seized and compelled him to carry the cross to Calvary.

The sons of Simon were disciples of Jesus, but he himself had not accepted the Savior. Afterward Simon was forever grateful for the privilege of bearing the cross of the Redeemer. The burden he was thus forced to carry became the means of his conversion. The events of Calvary and the words uttered by Jesus led Simon to accept Him as the Son of God.

When they arrived at the place of crucifixion, the soldiers bound the condemned men to the instruments of torture. The two thieves wrestled in the hands of those who stretched them upon the cross. But the Savior did not resist.

The mother of Jesus had followed Him on that terrible journey to Calvary. She longed to care for Him as He sank exhausted under His burden, but the soldiers would not allow her to.

At every step of the way she had looked for Him to display His God-given power and release Himself from the murderous throng. And now that they had reached the place of execution and she saw the thieves bound to the cross, she endured an agony of suspense!

Would He who had given life to the dead allow Himself to be crucified? Would the Son of God permit the Romans cruelly to slay Him? Must she give up her faith that He was the Messiah?

She saw His hands stretched upon the cross—those hands that had constantly reached out to bless the suffering. A soldier brought the hammer and the nails and drove the spikes through the tender flesh. The heartbroken disciples carried the fainting mother of Jesus away from the scene.

The Savior made no murmur of complaint. His face remained pale and serene, but great drops of sweat stood on His brow. Already His disciples had fled from the dreadful scene. He was treading the winepress alone (Isaiah 63:3).

As the soldiers went about their work, Jesus' thoughts shifted from His own sufferings to the terrible retribution that His persecutors must one day meet. He pitied them in their ignorance. "Father, forgive them, for they do not know what they do" (Luke 23:34), He prayed.

Christ was earning the right to become humanity's advocate and representative in the Father's presence. That prayer for His enemies embraced the world. It took in every sinner who had lived or should live, from the beginning of the world to the end of time.

Whenever we sin, it wounds Christ once again. For us He lifts His pierced hands before the Father's throne and says, "Forgive them, for they do not know what they do."

As soon they had Christ nailed to the cross, strong men lifted it and thrust it into the hole dug for it. The terrible jolt caused intense suffering to the Son of God.

Pilate then wrote an inscription in Latin, Greek, and Hebrew and placed it upon the cross above the head of Jesus, where all might see it. It read:

"Jesus of Nazareth, the King of the Jews" (John 19:19).

The religious leaders requested a different sign. The chief priests said:

"Do not write, 'The King of the Jews,' but, 'He said, "I am the King of the Jews"'" (verse 21).

But Pilate was angry with himself because of his former weakness. He also thoroughly despised the jealous and wicked rulers. So he answered, "What I have written, I have written" (verse 22).

The soldiers divided Jesus' clothing among themselves. One garment had been woven without a seam, so they could not easily tear it apart and share the pieces. They argued about who should have the whole garment. Finally they settled the matter by casting lots.

God's prophet had foretold that they would do this. He wrote:

"Dogs have surrounded Me; the congregation of the wicked has enclosed Me. They pierced My hands and My feet; . . . They divide My garments among them, and for My clothing they cast lots" (Psalm 22:16-18).

As soon as the soldiers raised Jesus on the cross, the priests, rulers, and scribes joined with the rabble in mocking and jeering the dying Son of God. "If You are the King of the Jews, save Yourself" (Luke 23:37).

"He saved others; Himself He cannot save. If He is the King of Israel, let Him now come down from the cross, and we will believe Him. He trusted in God; let Him deliver Him now if He will have Him; for He said, 'I am the Son of God'" (Matthew 27:42, 43).

"And those who passed by blasphemed Him, wagging their heads and saying, 'Aha! You who destroy the temple and build it in three days, save Yourself, and come down from the cross!'" (Mark 15:29, 30).

Christ could have left the cross. But if He had done this, we could never have been saved. For our sake He was willing to die.

"But He was wounded for our transgressions, He was bruised for our iniquities; the chastisement for our peace was upon Him, and by His stripes we are healed" (Isaiah 53:5).

24

Death of Christ

As He yielded up His life, Christ did not feel triumphant joy. Anguish tore His heart apart and gloom oppressed Him. But it was not the fear or the pain of death that caused His suffering. It was the crushing weight of the world's sin and a sense of separation from His Father's love. This was what broke the Savior's heart and resulted in His quick death.

Christ endured the agony that sinners will feel when they awake from death to realize the burden of their guilt, to know that they have forever separated themselves from the joy and peace of heaven.

Angels watched with amazement the despair that filled the Son of God. His mental anguish was so intense that He hardly felt the pain of the cross.

Nature itself expressed its sympathy with Christ. The sun had shone clearly

until midday, when suddenly it seemed to be blotted out. All about the cross hung a darkness as deep as the blackest midnight. This supernatural darkness lasted fully three hours.

A nameless terror seized the mob. Their cursing and insults ceased. Men, women, and children fell upon the earth in total terror.

Lightning occasionally flashed forth from the cloud, revealing the cross and the crucified Redeemer. All thought that their time of punishment had come.

At the ninth hour the darkness lifted from the people, but it still wrapped the Savior like a cloak. The lightning seemed to hurl itself at Him as He hung upon the cross. It was then that He exclaimed, "My God, My God, why have You forsaken Me?" (Matthew 27:46; Mark 15:34).

In the meantime the darkness had settled over Jerusalem and the plains of Judea. As all eyes gazed in the direction of the fated city, they saw the fierce lightning flashes of God's wrath directed toward it.

Suddenly the gloom lifted from the cross, and in clear trumpet-like tones that seemed to resound throughout creation, Jesus cried, "It is finished!" (John 19:30). "Father, 'into Your hands I commit My spirit'" (Luke 23:46).

A light encircled the cross, and the face of the Savior shone with a glory like that of the sun. He then bowed His head upon His breast and died.

The crowd about the cross stood paralyzed. Holding their

breath, they gazed upon the Savior. Again darkness settled upon the earth. People heard a hoarse rumbling like heavy thunder. A violent earthquake shook the ground.

The earthquake knocked the people down in heaps. Confusion and terror filled everyone. In the surrounding mountains rocks crashed down into the plains below. Tombs broke open, throwing many bodies out. Creation seemed to be shattering into atoms. Priests, rulers, soldiers, and people, mute with terror, sprawled upon the ground.

At the time of the death of Christ some of the priests were serving in the Temple at Jerusalem. They felt the shock of the earthquake. Just at that same moment the veil of the Temple separating the holy from the Most Holy Place ripped from top to bottom. The same hand that had written the words of doom upon the walls of Belshazzar's palace now tore the curtain. The Most Holy Place of the earthly sanctuary was no longer sacred. Never again would the presence of God overshadow that mercy seat. Never again would God show His acceptance or displeasure by the light or shadow in the precious stones in the breastplate of the high priest.

From now on the blood of the offerings in the Temple had no value. The Lamb of God, in dying, had become the sacrifice for the sins of the world.

When Christ died upon the cross of Calvary, His death threw open a new and living way for both Jew and Gentile alike.

Angels rejoiced as the Savior cried, "It is finished!" The great plan of redemption was to be carried out. Through a life of obedience the sons of Adam might be exalted finally to the presence of God.

Satan was defeated and knew that his kingdom was lost.

25

In Joseph's Tomb

The Roman government had condemned the Savior for treason. Persons put to death for that were buried in a place set apart for such criminals.

John shuddered at the thought of having the body of his beloved Master handled by the unfeeling soldiers, then buried in a dishonored grave. But he saw no way to prevent it, as he had no influence with Pilate.

At this trying time Nicodemus and Joseph of Arimathea came to the help of the disciples. Both men belonged to the Sanhedrin and were acquainted with Pilate. And both had wealth and influence. They were determined that the Savior's body should have an honorable burial.

Joseph went boldly to Pilate and asked for the body of Jesus. Pilate, after learning that Christ was really dead, granted his request.

While Joseph went to Pilate for the Savior's body, Nicodemus prepared for the burial. It was the custom in those times to wrap the bodies of the dead in linen cloths along with expensive ointments and sweet spices. So Nicodemus brought a costly gift of about 100 pounds of myrrh and aloes for the body of Jesus.

The most honored in all Jerusalem could not have received more respect in death. The humble followers of Jesus were astonished to see these wealthy leaders taking such an interest in the burial of their Master.

Sorrow at the death of Christ had overwhelmed the disciples. They forgot that He had told them that it would happen. Now they were without hope.

Neither Joseph nor Nicodemus had openly accepted the Savior while He was living. But they had listened to His teachings and had closely watched every step of His ministry. Although the disciples had forgotten the Savior's words foretelling His death, Joseph and Nicodemus remembered them well. The events of Jesus' death disheartened the disciples and shook their faith. But the same events convinced these two leaders that He was the true Messiah. Christ's death led Joseph and Nicodemus to take their stand firmly as believers in Him.

The help of these rich and honored men was greatly needed at this time. They could do for their dead Master what was impossible for the poor disciples.

Gently and reverently they, with their own hands, removed the body of Christ from the cross. Tears of sympathy streaked their faces as they looked upon His bruised and torn body.

Joseph owned a new tomb hewn in rock. He had built it for his own use, but he now prepared it for Jesus. The men wrapped the body, together with the spices Nicodemus had brought, in a linen sheet and carried the Redeemer to the tomb.

Although the Jewish leaders had succeeded in putting Christ to death, they could not rest easy. They well knew of His mighty power.

Some of them had stood by the grave of Lazarus and had seen Jesus bring the dead back to life. The rulers had heard Him say that He had power to lay down His life and to take it again. They trembled in fear that Christ would Himself rise from the dead and again appear before them.

Also they remembered that He had said, "Destroy this temple, and in three days I will raise it up" (John 2:19). The religious leaders knew that He was speaking about His own body.

Judas had told them that Christ had said to His disciples on their last journey to Jerusalem:

"Behold, we are going up to Jerusalem, and the Son of Man will be betrayed to the chief priests and to the scribes; and they will condemn Him to death, and deliver Him to the Gentiles to mock and to scourge and to crucify. And the third day He will rise again" (Matthew 20:18, 19).

Vividly they now remembered many things that He had said predicting His resurrection. No matter how much they wanted to, they could not forget these things. Like their father, the devil, they believed and trembled.

Everything declared to them that

Jesus was the Son of God. They could not sleep, for they were more worried about Him in His death than they had been during His life.

Bent on doing all they could to keep Him in the grave, they asked Pilate to have the tomb sealed and guarded until the third day. Pilate placed a band of soldiers at the command of the priests and told them, "'You have a guard; go your way, make it as secure as you know how.' So they went and made the tomb secure, sealing the stone and setting the guard" (Matthew 27:65, 66).

26

"He Is Risen"

The religious leaders had taken the greatest care to guard the Savior's tomb. They had closed the entrance with a great stone. Upon the stone the Roman seal had been placed in such a way that the stone could not be moved without breaking the seal.

Around the tomb stood the guard of Roman soldiers. They were to keep strict watch so that nothing would bother the body of Jesus. Some of them constantly paced back and forth in front of the tomb, while the others rested on the ground nearby.

But another guard also protected that tomb. Mighty angels from heaven were there. Any one of this angel guard could have overcome the whole Roman army.

The night preceding the morning of the first day of the week slowly came to an end, and the darkest hour, just before daybreak, had arrived.

God sent one of the most powerful angels from heaven to the tomb. His appearance was like lightning and his garments white as snow. He lighted the whole heavens with his glory.

The sleeping soldiers jolted awake and leaped to their feet. With awe and wonder they gazed at the open heavens and the brightness coming toward them.

The earth trembled and heaved as that powerful being from another world approached. He hurried on a joyful errand. The speed and power of his flight shook the world like a mighty earthquake. Soldiers, officers, and sentinels collapsed to the ground.

A third guard also surrounded the Savior's tomb. Evil angels were there. Because the Son of God had fallen in death, they claimed His body as the prey of him who has the power of death—the devil.

The angels of Satan wanted to make sure that no power could take Jesus from their grasp. But as the mighty being sent from the throne of God approached, they fled in terror.

The angel grabbed the great stone at the mouth of the tomb and rolled it away as if it had been just a pebble. Then with a voice that caused the earth to tremble, he cried, "Jesus, Son of God, come forth, Your Father calls You!"

Then He who had earned the power over death and the grave came forth from the tomb. Above the now-empty sepulchre He proclaimed, "I am the resurrection and the life." And the angel host bowed low in adoration before the Redeemer and welcomed Him with songs of praise.

Jesus left the tomb with the step of a conqueror. At His presence the earth reeled, the lightning flashed, and the thunder rolled.

An earthquake marked the hour when Christ laid down His life. Now an earthquake also witnessed the moment when He took it up in triumph.

Satan was bitterly angry that his angels had fled at the approach of the heavenly messenger. He had dared to hope that Christ would not take up His life again, that the plan of redemption would fail. But as he saw the Savior leave the tomb in triumph, all hope was lost. Satan now knew that his kingdom would have an end, and that he must finally be destroyed.

27

Go Tell My Disciples

Luke, in his account of the Savior's burial, speaks of the women who were with Him at His crucifixion. He says that "they returned and prepared spices and fragrant oils. And they rested on the Sabbath according to the commandment" (Luke 23:56).

The Savior had been buried on Friday, the sixth day of the week. The women prepared spices and ointments to embalm their Lord, then put them aside until the Sabbath had ended. They would not even embalm the body of Jesus upon the Sabbath.

"Now when the Sabbath was past," "very early in the morning, on the first day of the week, they came to the tomb when the sun had risen" (Mark 16:1, 2).

As they neared the garden, they were surprised to see the sky beautifully lighted up and the earth trembling beneath their feet. They rushed to the tomb and were still more astonished to find the stone rolled away and the Roman guard not there.

Mary Magdalene had been the first to reach the place. Seeing that the stone had been removed, she hurried away to tell the disciples. When the other women arrived, they noticed a light shining about the tomb and, looking in, saw that it was empty.

Suddenly they saw a young man in shining clothing sitting by the tomb. It was the angel who had rolled away the stone. In fear they turned to flee, but the angel said:

"Do not be afraid, for I know that you seek Jesus who was crucified. He is not here; for He is risen, as He said. Come, see the place where the Lord lay. And go quickly and tell His disciples that He is risen from the dead, and indeed He is going before you into Galilee; there you will see Him" (Matthew 28:5-7).

When the women again looked into the tomb, they saw another shining angel. He asked them:

"Why do you seek the living among the dead? He is not here, but is risen! Remember how He spoke to you when He was still in Galilee, saying, 'The Son of Man must be delivered into the hands of sinful men, and be crucified, and the third day rise again'" (Luke 24:5-7).

The angels then explained the death and resurrection of Christ. They reminded the women that Christ had told beforehand of His crucifixion and resurrection. These words of Jesus were now plain to them. With fresh hope and courage they hurried off to tell the glad news.

Mary had not been present during this incident, but she now returned with Peter and John. When they went back to Jerusalem, she stayed at the tomb. She could not bear to leave until she learned what had become of the body of her Lord. As she stood weeping she heard a voice:

"Woman, why are you weeping? Whom are you seeking?" (John 20:15).

Tears so blinded her that she did not notice who it was that spoke to her. She

thought it might be the gardener and said to him pleadingly, "Sir, if you have carried Him away, tell me where You have laid Him, and I will take Him away" (verse 15).

She thought that if this rich man's tomb was considered too honorable for her Lord, she herself would provide a place for Him. But now the voice of Christ Himself fell upon her ears. He said, "Mary!" (verse 16).

Quickly brushing her tears away, she saw the Savior. Forgetting that He had been crucified, in her joy she stretched forth her hands to Him, saying, "Rabboni!" (Teacher) (verse 16).

Jesus then said, "Do not cling to Me, for I have not yet ascended to My Father; but go to My brethren and say to them, 'I am ascending to My Father and your Father, and to My God and your God'" (verse 17).

Jesus refused to receive the homage of His people until He should know that the Father had accepted His sacrifice. He ascended to the heavenly courts and from God Himself heard the assurance that His atonement for the sins of humanity had been ample and that through His blood all might gain eternal life.

The Prince of life received all power in heaven and on earth. He returned to His followers in a world of sin, that He might give to them His power and glory.

28

Witnesses

Late in the afternoon of the day of the resurrection two of the disciples were on their way to Emmaus, a little town eight miles from Jerusalem.

They were perplexed over the events that had recently taken place. The reports of the women who had seen the angels and had met Jesus after His resurrection especially puzzled them.

Now they were returning to their home to meditate and pray. The men hoped they would gain some light about those matters that seemed so dark to them.

As they journeyed a stranger joined them, but they were so busy with their conversation that they hardly noticed His presence.

The two disciples were so burdened with grief that they wept as they traveled along. Christ's heart of love saw here a sorrow that He could comfort.

Disguised as a stranger, He began to talk with them. "But their eyes were restrained, so that they did not know Him. And He said to them, 'What kind of conversation is this that you have with one another as you walk and are sad?'

"Then the one whose name was Cleopas answered and said to Him, 'Are You the only stranger in Jerusalem, and have You not known the things which happened there in these days?'

"And He said to them, 'What things?'

"So they said to Him, 'The things concerning Jesus of Nazareth, who was a Prophet mighty in deed and word before God and all the people'" (Luke 24:16-19).

They then told what had taken place and repeated the account given by the women who had been at the tomb early that same morning. Then Jesus said:

"O foolish ones, and slow of heart to believe in all that the prophets have spoken! Ought not the Christ to have suffered these things and to enter into His glory?" (verses 25, 26).

"And beginning at Moses and all the Prophets, He expounded to them in all the Scriptures the things concerning Himself" (verse 27).

The disciples were silent from amazement and delight. They did not ask the stranger who He was. Instead, they listened eagerly as He explained to them Christ's mission.

Had the Savior first made Himself known to the disciples, they would have been satisfied. In the fullness of their joy they would have desired nothing more. But it was necessary for them to understand how all the symbols and prophecies of the Old Testament had foretold His mission. Their faith must be established upon them. Christ performed no miracle to convince them, but it was His first work to explain the Scriptures. They had looked upon His death as the destruction of all their hopes. Now He showed from the prophets that it was the very strongest evidence for their faith.

As He taught these disciples Christ showed the importance of the Old Testament as a witness to His mission. Many now reject the Old Testament, claiming that it is no longer of any use. But that is not Christ's teaching. So highly did

He value it, that at one time He said, "If they do not hear Moses and the prophets, neither will they be persuaded though one rise from the dead" (Luke 16:31).

The disciples reached their home as the sun was setting. Jesus "indicated that He would have gone farther" (Luke 24:28). But the disciples could not bear to part from the One who had brought them such joy and hope.

So they said to Him, "'Abide with us, for it is toward evening, and the day is far spent.' And He went in to stay with them" (verse 29).

The simple evening meal was soon ready. As His custom was, Christ took His place at the head of the table.

It was usually the duty of the head of the family to ask a blessing upon the food. But Christ placed

His hands upon the bread and blessed it. Suddenly the disciples realized who He was.

The act of blessing the food, the sound of the now-familiar voice, the prints of the nails in His hands—all proclaimed Him their beloved Master.

For a moment they sat spellbound. Then they arose to fall at His feet and worship Him. But at that moment He disappeared.

In their joy they forgot their hunger and weariness. They left the meal untasted and raced back to Jerusalem with the wonderful message of a risen Savior.

As they related these things to the other disciples, Christ Himself stood among them. Hands uplifted in blessing, He said, "Peace to you" (verse 36).

At first they were frightened. But when He had shown them the prints of the

nails in His hands and feet and had eaten in front of them, they believed. Faith and joy now took the place of unbelief and sorrow. With feelings that no words could express, they acknowledged their risen Savior.

The disciple Thomas had not been with them at this meeting. He refused to believe the reports about Jesus' resurrection. But after eight days Jesus appeared to the disciples again when Thomas was present.

On this occasion Christ again showed in His hands and feet the marks of the crucifixion. Immediately convinced, Thomas exclaimed, "My Lord and my God!" (John 20:28).

In the upper chamber Jesus again explained what the Scriptures had to say about Himself. Then He told His disciples that repentance and forgiveness of sins should be preached in His name among all nations, beginning at Jerusalem.

Before His ascension to heaven He said to them, "You shall receive power when the Holy Spirit has come upon you; and you shall be witnesses to Me in Jerusalem, and in all Judea and Samaria, and to the end of the earth" (Acts 1:8) "And lo, I am with you always, even to the end of the age" (Matthew 28:20).

You have been witnesses, He said, of My life of self-sacrifice in behalf of the world. You have seen that all who come to Me, confessing their sins, I freely accept. All who want to be, may be reconciled to God and have everlasting life.

To you, My disciples, I give this message of mercy. You are to take it to all nations, tongues, and peoples.

Even though you go to the farthest part of the world, I will be there with you. You may work in faith and confidence, because I will never forsake you.

The Savior's commission to the disciples involves all believers. It includes all those who accept Christ to the end of time. All who receive the life of Christ are to work for the salvation of their fellow human beings.

Not all can preach to congregations, but all can serve other individuals. We minister to others when we receive the suffering, help the needy, comfort the sorrowing, and tell the sinner of Christ's pardoning love. When we do that, we are all Christ's witnesses.

29

This Same Jesus

The Savior's work on earth was finished. The time had now come for Him to return to His heavenly home. He had overcome sin. Once again He would take His place by the side of His Father upon His throne of light and glory.

Jesus chose the Mount of Olives as the place of His ascension. Accompanied by the 11 disciples, He made His way to the mountain. But the disciples did not know that it would be their last time with their Master. As they walked up the steep slope the Savior gave them His parting instruction. Just before leaving them, He made that precious promise so dear to every one of His followers: "Lo, I am with you always, even to the end of the age" (Matthew 28:20).

They crossed the summit to the vicinity of Bethany. Here they paused. The disciples gathered about their Lord. Beams of light seemed to radiate from Him as He looked with love upon them. Words of the deepest tenderness were the last that fell upon their ears from the lips of the Savior.

With hands outstretched in blessing He slowly ascended into the sky. As He rose upward the awestruck disciples looked with straining eyes for the last glimpse of their Lord. A cloud of glory soon hid Him from their sight. At the same time there floated down to them the sweetest and most joyous music from the angel choir.

While the disciples were still gazing upward, voices that sounded like music now spoke to them. They turned and saw two angels in the shape of men. The angels said:

"Men of Galilee, why do you stand gazing up into heaven? This same Jesus, who was taken up from you into heaven, will so come in like manner as you saw Him go into heaven" (Acts 1:11).

The angels belonged to the group that had come to escort the Savior to His heavenly home. In sympathy and love for those left below, they had stayed to assure them that this separation would not last forever.

Jesus had promised to come again. He had told the disciples:

"Let not your heart be troubled; you believe in God, believe also in Me. In My Father's house are many mansions; if it were not so, I would have told you. I go to prepare a place for you. And if I go and prepare a place for you, I will come again and receive you to Myself; that where I am, there you may be also" (John 14:1-3).

The angels declared to the disciples that Christ would "so come in like manner" as they had seen Him go to heaven. He ascended bodily, and they saw Him as He left them and disappeared into the cloud. Soon He will return on a great white cloud, and "every eye will see Him" (Revelation 1:7).

Enoch testified, "Behold, the Lord comes with ten thousands of His saints, to execute judgment on all" (Jude 14).

Isaiah prophesied that the righteous will declare at His coming, "Behold, this is our God; we have waited for Him, and He will save us" (Isaiah 25:9).

The apostle Paul, describing the same scene, said:

"The Lord Himself will descend from heaven with a shout, with the voice of an archangel, and with the trumpet of God. And the dead in Christ will rise first. Then we who are alive and remain shall be caught up together with them in the clouds to meet the Lord in the air. And thus we shall always be with the Lord" (1 Thessalonians 4:16, 17).

Thus will our Savior come back to the earth to take for Himself forever those who have been loyal to Him.

30

Their Ascended Lord

When the disciples returned to Jerusalem, the people stared at them with amazement. Most had assumed that after the trial and crucifixion of their Master they would be downcast and ashamed. Their enemies expected to see sorrow and defeat in their expressions. Instead people saw only gladness and triumph. The disciples' faces glowed with a happiness not born of earth. They did not mourn over disappointed hopes, but were full of praise and thanksgiving to God.

With great rejoicing they told the wonderful story of Christ's resurrection and His ascension to heaven. Many believed what the disciples told them and accepted Jesus as their Savior.

The disciples no longer feared the future. They realized that the Savior was in

heaven and that He still cared for them. Christ's followers knew that He was pleading before God the merits of His blood. He was showing to the Father His wounded hands and feet as evidence of the price that He had paid for His redeemed.

And the disciples knew that He would come again with all the holy angels. Now they looked for this event with great joy and anticipation.

When Jesus passed from the sight of His disciples on the Mount of Olives, a heavenly host met Him with songs of joy and triumph. Then they escorted Him upward.

At the gates of the city of God a company of angels too large to count awaited His coming. As Christ approached heaven the angels accompanying Him triumphantly sang to those at its gates:

"Lift up your heads, O you gates!
And be lifted up, you everlasting doors!
And the King of glory shall come in" (Psalm 24:7).

The angels at the gates responded:

"Who is this King of glory?" (verse 8).

They did not say this because they didn't know who He was, but because they desired to hear the wonderful answer:

"The Lord strong and mighty,
The Lord mighty in battle.
Lift up your heads, O you gates!
Lift up, you everlasting doors!
And the King of glory shall come in" (verses 8, 9).

Again the waiting angels asked:

"Who is this King of glory?" (verse 10).

The escorting angels replied in melodious strains:

"The Lord of hosts,
He is the King of glory" (verse 10).

Then the gates of the city of God opened wide, and the angelic throng swept through them amid a burst of rapturous music.

All the heavenly host were waiting to honor their returned Commander. They waited for Him to take His place upon the throne of the Father.

But He could not yet receive the crown of glory and the royal robe. He had a request to present before the Father concerning His chosen ones on earth. Christ would not accept any honor until His church was justified and accepted before the universe.

Our Savior asked that where He is, there His people may be. If He is to have glory, they must share it with Him. Those who suffer for Him on the earth must reign with Him in His kingdom.

Christ pleaded for His church. He identified His interests with theirs. With a love stronger than death He advocated the rights and titles purchased by His blood.

The Father answered His appeal with the proclamation:

"Let all the angels of God worship Him" (Hebrews 1:6).

Joyfully the leaders of the heavenly host adored the Redeemer. The countless angels bowed before Him, and heaven echoed and reechoed with the glad shout:

"Worthy is the Lamb who was slain to receive power and riches and wisdom, and strength and honor and glory and blessing!" (Revelation 5:12).

Christ's followers are "accepted in the Beloved." In the presence of the heavenly host, the Father ratified the covenant made with Christ that He will receive repentant and obedient human beings, and will love them even as He loves His Son. Where the Redeemer is, there the redeemed shall be.

The Son of God had triumphed over the prince of darkness. He had conquered death and sin. Heaven rang with voices in lofty strains proclaiming:

"Blessing and honor and glory and power be to Him who sits on the throne, and to the Lamb, forever and ever!" (verse 13).

Events in the Ministry of Jesus

First Year	Place	Matthew	Mark	Luke	John
Baptism	Jordan River	3:13-17	1:9-11	3:21–23	1:29-34
Satan tempts	wilderness	4:1-11	1:12, 13	4:1-13	
First miracle	Cana				2:1-11
Meets Nicodemus	Jerusalem				3:1-21
Woman at well	Samaria				4:5-42
Heals official's son	Cana				4:46-54
People try to kill Jesus	Nazareth			4:16-30	

Second Year	Place	Matthew	Mark	Luke	John
Calls four fishers	Sea of Galilee	4:18-22	1:16-20	5:1-11	
Heals Peter's mother-in-law	Capernaum	8:14, 15	1:29-31	4:28, 29	
Begins preaching in Galilee	Galilee	4:23-25	1:35-39	4:42-44	
Matthew follows Jesus	Capernaum	9:9-13	2:13-17	5:27-32	
Chooses 12 disciples	Galilee	10:2-4	3:13-19	6:12-16	
Sermon on the Mount	Galilee	5:1-7:28		6:20-49	
Travels through Galilee	Galilee			8:1-3	
Tells parables about kingdom	Galilee	13:1-52	4:1-34	8:4-18	
Quiets the storm	Sea of Galilee	8:23-27	4:35-41	8:22-25	
Raises Jairus's daughter	Capernaum	9:18-26	5:21-43	8:40-56	
Sends out 12 disciples	Galilee	9:35-11:1	6.7-13	9:1-6	

Third Year	Place	Matthew	Mark	Luke	John
John the Baptist killed	Perea	14:1-12	6:14-29	9:7-9	
Feeding of 5,000	near Bethsaida	14:15-21	6:30-44	9:10-17	6:1-14
Walks on water	Sea of Galilee	14:24-27	6:45-52		6:16-21
Feeding of 4,000	Sea of Galilee	15:32-38	8:1-9		
Peter says Jesus Son of God	Caesarea Philippi	16:13-20	8:27-30	9:18-21	
Predicts His death	Caesarea Philippi	16:21-26	8:31-37	9:22-25	
Transfiguration	unknown	17:1-13	9:2-13	9:28-36	
Pays Temple tax	Capernaum	17:24-27			
Goes to Feast of Tabernacles	Jerusalem				7:11-52

The Story of Jesus

Third Year	Place	Matthew	Mark	Luke	John
Heals man born blind	Jerusalem				9:1-41
Visits Mary and Martha	Bethany			10:38-42	
Raises Lazarus from the dead	Bethany				11:1-44
Begins last trip to Jerusalem	Border road			17:11	
Blesses children	Transjordan	19:13-15	10:13-16	18:15-17	
Talks to rich young man	Transjordan	19:16-30	10:17-31	18:18-30	
Again predicts His death	near Jordan	20:17-19	10:32-34	18:31-34	
Heals blind Bartimaeus	Jericho	20:29-34	10:46-52	18:35-43	
Talks to Zacchaeus	Jericho			19:1-10	
Visits Mary and Martha	Bethany				11:55-12:1

Last Week

Event	Place	Day	Matthew	Mark	Luke	John
Triumphal entry	Jerusalem	Sunday	21:1-11	11:1-10	19:29-44	12:12-19
Curses fig tree	Jerusalem	Monday	21:18-22	11:12-14, 20-24		
Cleanses Temple	Jerusalem	Monday	21:12, 13	11:15-18	19:45-48	
Jesus challenged	Jerusalem	Tuesday	21:23-27	11:27-33	20:1-8	
Teaches in Temple	Jerusalem	Tuesday	21:28-23:39	12:1-44	20:9-21:36	
Feet anointed	Bethany	Tuesday	26:6-13	14:3-9	7:36-50	12:2-11
Plot against Jesus	Jerusalem	Wednesday	26:14-16	14:10, 11	22:3-6	
Last Supper	Jerusalem	Thursday	26:17-29	14:12-25	22:7-20	13:1-38
Comforts disciples	Jerusalem	Thursday				14:1-16:33
High priestly prayer						17:1-26
Gethsemane	Jerusalem	Thursday	26:36-46	14:32-42	22:40-46	
Arrest and trial	Jerusalem	Friday	26:47-27:26	14:43-15:15	22:47-23:25	18:2-19:16
Crucifixion	Golgotha	Friday	27:27-56	15:16-41	23:26-49	19:17-30
Burial	Garden Tomb	Friday	27:57-61	15:42-47	23:50-56	19:38-42
Resurrection	Garden Tomb	Sunday	28:1-15	16:1-11	24:1-12	20:18

Miracles of Jesus

	Matthew	Mark	Luke	John
Miracles of healing				
Man with leprosy	8:2-4	1:40-42	5:12, 13	
Roman centurion's servant	8:5-13		7:1-10	
Peter's mother-in-law	8:14, 15	1:30, 31	4:38, 39	
Gadarene demoniac(s)	8:28-34	5:1-17	8:26-37	
Paralyzed man	9:2-7	2:3-12	5:18-25	
Bleeding woman	9:20-22	5:25-34	8:43-48	
Two blind men	9:27-31			
Mute, demon-possessed man	9:32, 33			
Man with withered hand	12:10-13	3:1-5	6:6-10	
Demon-possessed, blind, and mute man	12:22		11:14	
Daughter of Canaanite woman	15:21-28	7:24-30		
Boy with demon	17:14-18	9:17-29	9:38-42	
Two blind men (with Bartimaeus)	20:29-34	10:46-52	18:35-43	
Deaf man with speech problem		7:31-37		
Man in synagogue		1:23-26	4:33-35	
Blind man at Bethsaida		8:22-26		
Crippled woman			13:11-13	
Man with dropsy			14:1-4	
10 lepers			17:11-19	
High priest's slave's ear			22:50, 51	
Official's son at Capernaum				4:46-54
Man at pool of Bethesda				5:1-9
Man born blind				9:1-7

	Matthew	Mark	Luke	John
Miracles over nature				
Calming storm	8:23-27	4:37-41	8:22-25	
Walking on water	14:24-27	6:48-51		6:19-21
Feeding 5,000	14:15-21	6:35-44	9:12-17	6:5-13
Feeding 4,000	15:32-38	8:1-9		

The Story of Jesus

	Matthew	Mark	Luke	John
Fish with coin	17:24-27			
Withered fig tree	21:18-22	11:12-14, 20-24		
Catch of fish			5:4-11	
Water into wine				2:1-11
Second catch of fish				21:1-11

Miracles over death

	Matthew	Mark	Luke	John
Jairus's daughter	9:18, 19, 23-25	5:22-24, 38-43	8:41, 42, 49-56	
Son of widow of Nain			7:11-15	
Lazarus				11:1-44

Parables of Jesus

Parable	Matthew	Mark	Luke
Lamp under basket	5:14, 15	4:21	8:16; 11:33
Wise and foolish builders	7:24-27		6:47-49
New cloth on old coat	9:16	2:21	5:36
New wine in old wineskins	9:17	2:22	5:37, 38
Sower and soils	13:3-8, 18-23	4:3-8, 14-20	8:5-8, 11-15
Weeds	13:24-30, 36-43		
Mustard seed	13:31, 32	4:30-32	13:18, 19
Yeast	13:33		13:20, 21
Hidden treasure	13:44		
Valuable pearl	13:45, 46		
Net	13:47-50		
Master of household	13:52		
Lost sheep	18:12-14		15:4-7
Unforgiving servant	18:23-34		
Vineyard laborers	20:1-16		

Parable	Matthew	Mark	Luke
Two sons	21:28-32		
Tenants	21:33-44	12:1-11	20:9-18
Wedding feast	22:2-14		
Fig tree	24:32-35	13:28, 29	21:29-31
Faithful and wise servant	24:45-51		12:42-48
10 bridesmaids	25:1-13		
Talents	25:14-30		19:12-27
Sheep and goats	25:31-46		
Growing seed		4:26-29	
Watchful servants		13:34-37	12:35-40
Creditor			7:41-43
Good Samaritan			10:30-37
Needy friend			11:5-8
Rich fool			12:16-21
Barren fig tree			13:6-9
Lowest seat at the feast			14:7-14
Great dinner			14:16-24
Cost of discipleship			14:28-33
Lost coin			15:8-10
Prodigal son			15:11-32
Dishonest manager			16:1-8
Rich man and Lazarus			16:19-31
Master and slave			17:7-10
Persistent widow			18:2-8
Pharisee and tax collector			18:10-14